CONTEMPORARY
RUSSIAN COMPOSERS

M. P. BELAYEF.

PATRON and PUBLISHER of MODERN RUSSIAN MUSIC

After the portrait by J. E. Repin.

CONTEMPORARY RUSSIAN COMPOSERS

By

M. MONTAGU-NATHAN

GREENWOOD PRESS, PUBLISHERS
WESTPORT, CONNECTICUT

123089

Originally published in 1917
by Cecil Palmer & Hayward, London

First Greenwood Reprinting 1970

Library of Congress Catalogue Card Number 72-109795

SBN 8371-4285-7

Printed in the United States of America

TO
S. W. PRING

CONTENTS

LIST OF ILLUSTRATIONS

PREFACE

WHEN planning the material of my HISTORY OF
RUSSIAN MUSIC—the first collective work on the
subject in the English language—it was my intention to include therein a reference to every
Russian composer of distinction ; its omissions
are accidental.

In the present work, however, I have deemed
it expedient to make a selection. In so doing I
have been actuated by two motives : to meet, on
the one hand, a demand for the life-story and a
critical review of the work of certain Russian
composers whose names figure frequently in our
concert programmes ; and, on the other, to
create a demand for a hearing of compositions
which are already the subject of much comment
in Russia, but which are as yet unknown to the
British public.

The reader who considers that I have allotted
my space disproportionately is asked to bear in
mind that his objections are the result of a difference of opinion between himself and the author
as to the present needs of the public in regard to
the matter ; he will not be justified in assuming
the following chapters to be intended in every

case as a comprehensive account of the composer and his work. It should be obvious that the public would be disinclined to follow the author through an exhaustive analysis of the work of any composer whose name it had never hitherto seen and none of whose works had ever been performed in Britain. The treatment of the younger pioneers is therefore to be viewed by the reader who happens to have specialized as being deliberately compendious rather than cursory, and not, at all events, as representing any disposition on my part to underrate their significance.

In regard to the title of this volume I may point out that it is hardly possible to observe the letter of the qualification "Contemporary." My readers will no doubt have perceived that certain living composers are writing music which is far less advanced in style than that of other composers who are dead. While entitling this work CONTEMPORARY RUSSIAN COMPOSERS, I have accorded a preferential treatment to music which has some claim to be considered as reflecting the spirit of our time, and I have assumed the prerogative of ignoring all composers who do not write contemporary music and of dealing briefly with examples whose content is in no further need of exegesis.

If this work is successful in convincing the musical public that Russian Music is no nine

Preface

days' wonder, and that the genius of a nation which has only of recent years been admitted to the musical Concert of Europe is likely to make itself felt, not as a conquering but as an inspiring force in every realm where music is received as a refining art, its compilation will not have been in vain.

A general expression of indebtedness is due to the many Russian authors whose writings I have consulted, and to Messrs. J. and W. Chester & Co., through whose courtesy my examination of the products of the modern Russian School has been facilitated.

Harpsden Gate,
   Henley-on-Thames.
    October, 1916.

A SURVEY OF RUSSIAN MUSICAL HISTORY

B

CONTEMPORARY RUSSIAN COMPOSERS

CHAPTER I

A SURVEY OF RUSSIAN MUSICAL HISTORY

(1)

THE history of Russian art-music proper, unlike that of the other nations of our hemisphere, does not take us back into the remoter centuries. But if we are to appreciate the full significance of the greatest products of the Russian school of creative musicians, it is to the earliest historical records of their race that we must turn.

The reason of this is twofold. Viewed from the literary standpoint, Russian art-music is clearly seen to have its root in national and political history ; in examining it as music we are not long in discovering that the first chapter of the volume, which in the last hundred years has so completely altered its character, was written in the far-distant age of minstrelsy. Perusing the annals and products of that golden age of national music—the period beginning with Glinka's initiation of the nationalistic ideal, continued with so much energy by the staunch little band of idealists of

3

which Balakiref was the recognized leader in the early 'sixties, and ending with the meteoric descent of a fully-fledged school upon an unsuspecting and somewhat self-complacent Europe—we observe repeated instances of a reflection of bardic institutions.

The more we study the pages of Glinka's *Russlan and Ludmilla*, of Borodin's *Prince Igor*, of Rimsky-Korsakof's *Sadko*, or of Stravinsky's *The Rite of Spring*, the less inclined we are to be satisfied with the message of their music alone. We become possessed of a desire for a knowledge of these legends and myths to which they so frequently refer, for information bearing upon the origins of that folk-lore and song in which Russian opera and symphonic music abound.

Russian musical history resolves itself into a chronicle in which we see the alternate rise and fall of native folk-melody. Following upon the age of minstrelsy, when, in the tenth century, the troubadour was a real power in the land, came the introduction of Christianity, bringing with it a strenuous battle waged by the priests of the new faith against the paganistic spirit of the Slavonic legends and folk-songs. " Owing either to their fidelity to Oriental asceticism, to the Christian spirit of the initial centuries, or to the necessity of keeping a hold upon a people freshly converted and still impregnated with paganism," says

4

Patouillet in his *Le Théâtre de Mœurs Russes*, "the Orthodox Church watched anxiously over the social and domestic life of the nation and treated every profane recreation as a sin . . ." Continuing, the Frenchman quotes the "old moralist," whose words are given by Milioukof in his *Sketch for a History of Russian Culture*. "Laughter does not edify or redeem us, it dispels and destroys edification ; laughter grieves the Holy Spirit, it banishes the virtues, for it causes forgetfulness of death and eternal punishment."

But the priests, despite their arduous efforts, were unable to stamp out the songs and ceremonials which they viewed with so much disfavour ; they were obliged to make a compromise. They pursued the wise course of relinquishing the futile policy of total destruction, instituting in its stead the plan of rendering these popular amusements as far as possible innocuous by introducing references which were somewhat better in keeping with ecclesiastical precept. If they were not entirely successful, if the guardians of folk-song —the gusslars and skomorokhs—were secretly encouraged by the nobles to whose pleasures they ministered, the Church was at least able to maintain for a time an appearance of discipline. Gradually, it seems, the clandestinely nurtured music of the soil emerged from the condition in which the ascetics had placed it, and proceeded to enjoy its long-sought and hard-won freedom with a goodwill which expressed itself in a manner that once more—and this time with greater justice—incurred the displeasure of the Church.

(2)

This process of ebb and flow was repeated in the succeeding centuries. The son of the first Romanof was responsible, through his patronage, for another ebullition of secular entertainments which, though not altogether devoid of licentiousness, were at all events instrumental in reviving a tradition. But for many years after this it was only the skeleton of a tradition. With the accession of Peter the Great came that influx of alien musicians who streamed through the " window opened into Europe " by that pioneer among sovereigns and monarch among pioneers, bringing with them influences that were to force native song once again into obscurity. The foreign musical idiom, while contributing to the cultivation of music as an art worthy of respect, diverted the attention of nobles and people alike from their own rich store of melody. The power of the alien grew year by year. In the reign of the Empress Anne, which began in 1732, the direction of the nation's music fell into the hands of Francesco Araya, a Neapolitan who had relinquished the honours bestowed upon him at home to gain fresh laurels, but according to Sir Arthur Helps [1] the responsibility of instruction in court circles was entrusted to a German. The Italian domination continued during the reign of Elizabeth Petrovna, Araya remaining at the head of musical affairs. But he now encountered rivalry from a company of French actors whose performances alternated with those of Araya's operatic troupe. Whether this divided patronage impelled the Italian to seek a means of ingratiating himself more firmly with his Russian following is not clear; it was subsequent to Elizabeth's installation of these competing Frenchmen that Araya instituted the innovation of opera in the vernacular.

But, as will readily be understood, the music remained thoroughly Italian in style, and the opera itself, although its text was by a Russian, had for its subject that of Mozart's *La Clemenza di Tito*, and was consequently not even the quasi-Russian product that was offered to succeeding generations. It is something of a mystery that a later work of Araya's on the subject of *Cephalus and Procris* should have been dubbed by its composer "the first opera in the Russian tongue," for its text by Soumarokhof was apparently of later date than Volkhof's version of the Italian plot above

[1] *Ivan de Biron, or the Russian Court in the Middle of Last Century.* 1874.

7

referred to. Araya's sub-heading avoids reference to the Greek subject, and certainly the music, which might be mistaken for that of any Italian of the period, appears to contain nothing that peculiarly fits it for its association with Ovid's Athenian princess.

(3)

With Catharine the Great, however, the national element began once more to obtain a somewhat firmer foothold on the first rung of the ladder it subsequently climbed. The Northern Semiramis is not to be given the credit for this. She gave sanction to a continuance of the Italian régime, and not being very confident of her own powers of judgment is said to have submitted the works of one of the most promising native musicians of her reign to the scrutiny of the favoured alien.

Her appetite for serious music seems to have grown in the eating, for while at first she was bored by Grand Opera, which she described in a letter to Grimm as being " somewhat difficult to digest," she is said to have regretted that the laws of the Orthodox Church would not permit of the spiritual music of Sarti being used for worship because it was instrumental.

At this epoch the Italians appear to have regained the supreme favour, and although such musicians as Galuppi, Sarti and Martini undoubtedly contributed to an improvement of musical affairs in Russia, they wielded their power in rather tyrannical fashion.

To Fomin (1741-1800), a native musician, fell at once the indignity of being under the surveillance of the alien, and the honour of writing the first real attempt at genuine Russian opera. *Aniouta*, the first of his numerous works, owed some of its success, says Cheshikin,[1] to the sallies of its librettist, Popof, against the feudal system. A similar tendency is noticeable in the text of the exceedingly popular *Wizard-Miller*, in which its compiler, Ablessimof, indulged in what Cheshikin styles a democratic method of thought, " expressed nevertheless with extreme caution." But the music, we are assured, played a not unimportant part in the success of the opera, although it is judged by the above-mentioned historian as rather amateurish, and as showing a want of experience in the technique of composition.

And, indeed, it would seem that most of the operas produced at this time by compatriots of Fomin, such as Paskievich and Matinsky, are not to be considered as having contributed very much towards the emancipation of their art. We have the sanction of Krouglikof for dismissing them as pseudo-national manifestations—works consisting

[1] *History of Russian Opera.*

9

largely of popular tunes, " treated strictly according to the Western recipe."

(4)

The real cause of the comparative slowness of
the development of musical nationalism is to be
found in the conditions under which it was being
nurtured. The movement may be characterized
as artificial ; the Russian people could hardly be
expected to demand the enfranchisement of a
native product when society as a whole averted
its gaze from everything of the sort. But a
change, partly the result of circumstance and
partly due to human endeavour, was soon to set
in. During the brief reign of the ill-fated Paul,
there came to Petrograd a young Venetian,
Catterino Cavos by name, who, at the age of 23,
was already at the head of a travelling operatic
troupe. Invited with his players to the Russian
capital by Prince Yousouppof, in 1798, he remained in Russia until his death in 1842, performing during that time a very great service to the
native music-drama. The aptness of Krouglikof's
metaphor, when he describes Cavos as having
" tilled the soil " of Russian opera so that it was
ready for *A Life for the Tsar* and *Russlan and
Ludmilla*—the seeds of operatic nationalism later
sown by Glinka—is the more easy to appreciate

when we observe among the titles of the dramatic works written by the industrious Italian such names as *Ilya the Hero*, *Dobrinya Nikitich* and *Ivan Soussanin*. The success of the last-named, when produced in 1815, was not by any means entirely due to the merit of its music ; the nature of Prince Shakovsky's text must surely have been a great factor, but the most important of all was the crushing defeat of Napoleon and the conflagration that in the year 1812 had contributed so largely to his ultimate downfall.

For in the burning of Moscow we are bound to recognize the cause of the earliest manifestation of that racial consciousness and pride, that wave of patriotism on which Russian art first floated towards the glories it has since attained. Of Pushkin's precursors it is often said that they tuned the instrument (the Russian tongue) on which the great national poet played. We may consider that it was Cavos who showed Glinka what tunes to play. It is for his manner of playing them that we pay tribute to the composer of *A Life for the Tsar*.

Of Glinka's contemporary, A. N. Verstovsky, the composer of *Askold's Tomb*, it may be said that with this opera he also paved the way, not for the actual composition of the work but for the presentation of *A Life for the Tsar* before the Russian people. In Verstovsky's famous and still quite popular contribution to the Russian operatic repertoire is to be remarked a successful attempt at rendering native song in a national manner. Where it differs from Glinka's great work, which was produced some fifteen months later, is in its general musical workmanship, on the one hand— Verstovsky, though a prolific composer, remained conspicuously lacking in technical matters—and, on the other, in the substance of its plot. While Zagoskin's novel, from which the libretto is derived, was of an historical nature, its subject has not the compelling interest of that of Glinka's opera. The story told by the latter is one which makes an immediate appeal to every Russian, while the name of Askold evokes for the average opera-goer only a vague reminiscence of historical knowledge acquired under pressure. But in the music of *Askold's Tomb* is something that is entirely in accord with the popular taste, not merely of the generation which witnessed its production but of those which succeeded. "Who," asks Sergei Aksakof, in his biography of Zagoskin, "does not know it, love it and sing it?" We may thus award to Verstovsky the honour of being by no means the least, though virtually the last, of the Russian composers of the preparatory period which leads up to the real inauguration of Russian musical nationalism.

(5)

The tradition of musical nationalism, hitherto mooted in rather half-hearted fashion, and later to be advocated with such passionate enthusiasm by the Young Russian School, was really established by Glinka. It is by studying his first and more popular work, *A Life for the Tsar*, that we are able to estimate the measure of progress towards a national style made by his precursors. For in *A Life for the Tsar*, despite its commendable neglect of crude folk-song, its composer's attempt to achieve an amalgamation of folk and art-music, his introduction of the native method of choral accompaniment and the many national touches, we receive a fairly strong reminder of the alien influences which Glinka was striving to combat.

The many nationalistic features—the modal character of the melodies, the contrapuntal choral imitations, the subtle use of the patriotic leading-motive, the insertion of passages in which the music is made to suggest the balalaika and the several allusions to historical and pseudo-historical episodes in the libretto—all these interest us and indicate the distance already traversed since the composition of those rather *naïf* essays in musical nationalism which were made in the preceding generation ; but we, who in the twentieth century are making a first acquaintance with the music of this, to Russians, almost sacred opera, we who have not been brought up to regard it with something like our reverential attitude towards Handel's *Messiah*, are inclined to wonder how any Russian can overlook certain instances of what to us appears an undiluted Italian manner.

If we find ourselves at first unable to understand in what lies the cause of the enthusiasm perennially aroused by this opera in the land of its origin, we need only inquire how the greater part of the classic musical literature would fare with us if it were introduced afresh, without the aid of our established esteem of it as the work of a great master ; we need only remember that the glamour of the earlier impression of *A Life for the Tsar* is perpetuated by its plot ; and if we desire to appraise this work in such manner as to arrive at a proper estimate of its value as a stimulus to the ardent nationalists for whom it served as a model, it behoves us to compare its form and substance with the works of Glinka's precursors ; then shall we see why Glinka spoke of an opera that should make his countrymen " feel at home," and then shall we be able to understand the musical historian's claim that the name of Glinka should have a significance equal to that of Pushkin in literature and somewhat greater than that of Brioullof in painting. It will then be readily agreed that Glinka was not the least worthy member of that curious trinity of the early nineteenth century.

(6)

But it must not be supposed that in *A Life for the Tsar* Glinka put forth every effort of which he was capable, leaving nothing further in the shape of a contribution to the nationalist treasury. In his second opera, *Russlan and Ludmilla*, and in his orchestral works, we find material which appears to have had an even greater influence upon the many descendants of this " Father of Russian Music " than the musical innovations and the intensely stirring plot of *A Life for the Tsar*. Compared with the latter, *Russlan* is to be reckoned vastly inferior from the dramatic point of view, and it is not without examples of that Italianism which Glinka had assimilated both at home and abroad. But in two particulars it marks a distinct epoch in the history of Russian music. It introduced the fantastic element in dignified surroundings, thus founding a tradition which seems in no danger of dying out, and its indication of the value of Eastern colour rendered a service that is inestimable. We have already referred to the metaphorical asseveration that Peter the Great opened a window into Europe.

Of one of Russia's greatest poets it is remarked that he annexed the Caucasus to Russian literature. And we may say, with all justice, that to Glinka we owe those gorgeous feasts of Oriental music that have since been placed before us by his successors. It is impossible to place the output of the modern Russians in a proper focus without bearing in mind at all times the nature of Glinka's legacy. As was pointed out by Prince Odoyevsky, *Russlan and Ludmilla* was not a mere " magic " opera ; that vein had already been exploited by his forerunners ; it was an opera in the style of the Russian fairy-tale, an opera-legend. In a poetic passage he acclaims Glinka as a mighty genius who has not only collected for us all the varied racial characteristics of the Orient, but has set them to music. " That the influence of *Russlan and Ludmilla* is responsible for such creations as have since been given to the world by Dargomijsky, Borodin, Rimsky-Korsakof and Stravinsky, can easily be grasped by anyone conversant with the history of music in Russia prior to and since the time of Glinka. Such operas as Rimsky-Korsakof's *Kashchei*, *Tsar Saltan*, *The Snow-Maiden*, *Sadko* and *Kitej*, and Stravinsky's ballet, *The Fire-Bird*, have all a foundation in a folk-lore in which the supernatural predominates. But there are other elements than this to support this opera's claim to the distinction of being a pioneer work. . . . Glinka perceived the advantage that would accrue to the art-nationalist who should think imperially, and his adoption of this principle has endowed Russian music with a source of melody that has since been heavily drawn upon. Opera is not the only region in which the benefit of Glinka's policy has been felt. Balakiref's piano fantasia, *Islamey*—a veritable epic of the Orient—Borodin's *In the Steppes of Central Asia*, and Rimsky-Korsakof's *Sheherazade*, all owe their inspiration to *Russlan and Ludmilla*. In each case a sensibility to Eastern colour was inherent; but the impulse to express the Orient in music originated in Glinka's example."[1]

Nor does his legacy to Russian music end here. Seeking to provide for the public of his day a form of symphonic music that would make a smaller demand upon its patience than the traditional symphony of three and four movements in length, he wrote the *Spanish Caprice*, the first of a series of short orchestral fantasies, and, thanks partly to the sanction and encouragement of Liszt —a warm supporter of the " Young Russian School "—this type of one-movement work was subsequently developed on a generous scale. To his search for and employment of the folk-song of Spain, the Spaniards owe the resuscitation in art-music of their now familiar popular melodies. The

[1] *Glinka*. Masters of Russian Music Series. Constable & Co., Ltd.

C   17

similar service rendered to his own country is estimated by Tchaikovsky in the following passage from his diary : " Without intending to compose anything beyond a simple humorous trifle, he has left us a little masterpiece, every bar of which is the outcome of enormous creative power. Half a century has passed since then, and many Russian symphonic works have been composed. . . . The germ of all this lies in his *Kamarinskaya*, as the oak-tree lies in the acorn."

(7)

In Alexander Sergeyevich Dargomijsky (1813-69) we have the immediate successor of Glinka. This composer is described by Krouglikof as being a man of brilliant talent rather than of genius. With this estimate those who view the work of Dargomijsky in a proper perspective are bound to disagree, and must surely perceive, on the contrary, that the composer of *Roussalka* and *The Stone Guest*, while possessing only a moderate musical talent, had that penetrating insight into truths that are hidden from the average mind, which we call genius.

In order to appreciate the quality of Dargomijsky's genius and to discern in what direction it was applied, we have only to recall the extent to which our own native drama has been emancipated since the recognition of that by-product of the Ibsenite reforms, the simplification of the stage-play. It is said that a great Victorian editor, when considering the appointment of a dramatic critic to his staff, averred that in his view the indispensable qualification for such a post should be that the applicant should never previously have entered a theatre.

Dargomijsky's merit lies not so much in his music as in its composer's appreciation of a need for the reform of opera. It is, therefore, necessary that we should possess some knowledge of the operatic world from the conditions of which Dargomijsky desired that opera should be rescued.

"In those days," writes the prophetess of Russian Music in Western Europe,[1] " the reformative efforts of Gluck had been completely forgotten and Italian opera ruled the world. And what was the form of these Italian operas? An amalgamation of detached pieces, all cut after the same pattern and invariably made up either of two parts : an andante and an allegro ; or of three parts, an andante between two allegros. In each of these parts, especially in the allegros, the principal melody returned in the shape of a refrain—the more commonplace the better—during which the hero strode from back to front or from side to side

---

[1] *César Cui.* Esquisse Critique. Comtesse de Mercy-Argenteau. Paris. 1888.

of the stage. The recitatives were often interminable and inconceivably inane ; and nothing
in the world, no kind of dramatic episode or even
catastrophe, could bring about a modification of
these forms. If the hero received a public insult,
instead of taking immediate punitory measures,
he would form up in a row with the rest of the
stage company, join them in singing a long andante
and then proceed to run the varlet through.
Choruses thought nothing of shouting frenziedly,
' Let us rush to the revenge ' without budging an
inch, etc."

Having paid homage to Glinka in the composition of his popular legendary opera *Russalka*,
Dargomijsky proceeded to turn from the consideration of the national element in music-drama
to that of the *rational*. The musical setting of a
dramatic text was no longer to be a succession of
tunes loosely strung together, nor the performance
to partake of the nature of a "concert in costume";
the text, instead of being the work of a journey-
man librettist, must be worthy to form part of a
dignified whole. In *Russalka* we discover already
an endeavour to construct an opera which should
break away from the approved artificial operatic
forms, an effort to reproduce conversation not in
conventional but in natural recitatives ; in *The
Stone Guest*, a musical setting of the Statue
episode in *Don Juan*, we see music elevated to the

rank of drama, and we are shown moreover that in the Dargomijskian formula there is no suggestion, as in Wagner's, of a tyranny in the behaviour of the promoted art. The music respects the drama. In Pushkin's text, which Dargomijsky set without alteration, there is no " crowd " ; in the musical setting the composer dispenses with a chorus.

It is not because of any loveliness in its music that *The Stone Guest* became a model for the reformers of the " Young Russian School," for the Italian verists, for the composer of *Pelléas et Mélisande*, but because in it there was, for the first time since Gluck's effort, an endeavour to re-establish the dignity of the musico-dramatic art. And when we remember that Dargomijsky's cry, " the sound must represent the word," and his demand for " the truth "—in song no less than in opera—were uttered without knowledge either of Wagner or of Ibsen, whose work had not yet begun, we can hardly deny to him the attribute of genius.

(8)

It was upon the initiatory labours of Glinka and Dargomijsky—the introduction of patriotic nationalism, folk-lore, fantasy and Orientalism by the former, and of dramatic and musical rationalism by the latter—that the " Young Russian School " was founded.

But whereas the awakening of nationalistic feeling, and its operatic manifestation, *A Life for the Tsar*, were due to the stirring events of the Napoleonic invasion, the desire to be natural, the craving for simplicity and for truth in all things, even in music, was engendered by the great Liberation of 1861. The spirit of individual liberty which inspired the junior characters in Turgenief's *Virgin Soil* was the impulse from which sprang the energies of the young group of reformers in the musical world.

The socialistic outlook of the 'sixties is as clearly reflected in the music of that period as it is in its art and literature. Literature, art and music were henceforth to be not for art's but for life's sake. Encouraged by such writers as Chernishevsky and Herzen, and by the realistic painters, Repin and Vereshchagin, our "Young Russian School" made known its view that music, too, might take its place in the scheme of personal enfranchisement.

And the musician-participants in this general movement towards "simplification"—already provided with examples of the historico-national, legendary and fantastic types of opera, but all contained in an operatic form which was primarily lyrical—were now to be given a model of realistic music-drama. That model was Dargomijsky's *The Stone Guest*.

The Young Russian group did not owe the

transmission of the inspiration it received from Glinka entirely to Dargomijsky. When Balakiref, the leader of the " Five,"[1] came as a young man to Petrograd, he lost no time in seeking out the composer of *A Life for the Tsar* and, visiting him at Tsarskoe Selo, where he was then living in semi-retirement, speedily established himself in the great man's favour. Glinka saw in Balakiref the man who was destined to carry on the campaign of Russian musical nationalism, which he had so fittingly inaugurated with his first epoch-making opera.

César Cui, the first recruit to the new movement, should perhaps be considered as having shared with Balakiref the burden of its foundation, for although he was only a theoretical nationalist —there would seem to have been a conflict between hereditary instincts and acquired views—his writings on behalf of the " Invincible Band " and its propaganda were of no little service in combating certain hostile forces at home and in dispelling misconceptions abroad. Borodin, in virtue of his labours in the social world, was well qualified to take a part in their councils. Furthermore, his musical gift, though not of a nature allowing of an emulation of Dargomijsky's naturalism,

---

[1] Balakiref, Cui, Borodin, Moussorgsky and Rimsky-Korsakof, the prime movers in the musical nationalist movement, are collectively known as "The Five," "The Kouchka" or "Mighty Little Heap," and "The Invincible Band."

contributed greatly to the perpetuation of the epic type of opera to which Glinka's *Russlan and Ludmilla* and his own *Prince Igor* conform, while his Eastern descent impelled him to use richer colouring than that of the rather *naïf* Orientalism of *Russlan*.

(9)

In Moussorgsky, the spiritual conversion of the nation is most strongly typified. Coming in contact with Dargomijsky at an impressionable age, he soon became dissatisfied both with the society by which, as a smart guardsman, he had been surrounded, and the music affected by such a circle. Of the " Five " he alone appears to have possessed the true seer's vision. His art is to be described as an expression of socialism in simultaneous relation to people and to music. Music was for him a means of human intercourse, but he was not prepared to entrust this function to any but naturalistic music. In opera, as in song, he was a close follower of his master. His dramatic, as well as his vocal works, are informed by that steadfast desire for naturalness which Dargomijsky seems to have been the first to awaken in him. Far more than either Balakiref, Cui or Borodin, Moussorgsky reflects the spirit of the 'sixties in Russia ; his works are in much closer touch with the literature and the painting of that period. They show us that although he was regarded with some alarm by his friends as a revolutionary, his ideals were of a kind that could not fail, when realized, to promote the evolution of the musical art. He transcended their " programme " because he saw the need not merely for the alteration of the function of music but of its constitution. He perceived that progress and music were in a sense interchangeable terms, that emotion is a symptom of progress, that music is the special language of emotion and that the vocation of the artist-musician is to seek the interpretation of humanity in terms of the present.

A study of Moussorgsky's life, works and utterances leads one to imagine that he considered it the paramount duty of a musician to adopt towards music an attitude of conservatism very different from that which the customary use of the term suggests, a conservatism designed to conserve in music a spirit of spontaneity, thus preventing any danger of a conventionalization of musical expression.

Viewed in relation to Glinka, Moussorgsky is seen to have followed his precursor's footsteps in choosing subjects of nationalistic import ; this he has done in such operas as *Boris Godounof* and *Khovanshchina* ; it is in his forms and in his means of expression that he is the whole-hearted disciple of Dargomijsky. In his songs we see the desire for " the truth above all things." Neither the Orientalism nor the fantasy of *Russlan* has a large share in his music, but certain sporadic instances may be observed in the Persian ballet of *Khovansh-china* and the *Baba-Yaga* number in his musical representation of Hartmann's pictures. But to view Moussorgsky in the proper perspective as an artist we are obliged to go to the completed *Boris Godounof* as the finished product, and to his abortive setting of Gogol's *The Match-Maker* as the skeleton or bare framework on which his art is based. In the latter we have an earnest of Moussorgsky's intentions as an artist, but the former shows us the profound humanity of the man.

(10)

The advent of Rimsky-Korsakof, the youngest of the group—at that time a naval cadet—can hardly have been looked upon by Balakiref and his followers as a matter of very great artistic import-ance. It is true that Balakiref took an immediate liking for the youth, apparently due in some degree to the latter's reverence for the extraordinary gifts possessed by his newly-found master. But, as Korsakof tells us in his Memoirs, his own musical attainments were at that time exceedingly slender, and further, as Borodin's attitude towards music was that of a dilettante and as Moussorgsky's was informed by an indifference to the necessity for study, Balakiref and Cui were looked upon as in every way superior to these three tyros. Yet neither of the two leaders was fully equipped for leadership, and it would seem that Balakiref's knowledge of the orchestra and Cui's experience of opera and song rendered each of the pair the complement of the other. What caused the earlier members of the group to regard the latest and youngest recruit as a mere novice was that not only was he entirely ignorant of musical theory but that he had no shining gift, such as had Moussorgsky, as an executant. How could they be expected to foresee that this humble member of the brotherhood would become the most prolific composer and the one who, in his output, would unite all the streams opened up by thé initiatory effort of Glinka with something of the realism and the humour and all the sincerity of Dargomijsky? And this is not the sum of Rimsky-Korsakof's achievement. By his resolve to make a thorough study of the theoretical aspect of music, with which his comrades' acquaintance was far from exhaustive, he was eventually able to supplement and even to eclipse the efforts of Cui in upholding the banner of nationalism against the onslaughts of a very determined opposition. By

27

passively dissociating himself from the " mere amateurs " of the much disdained group, he proved that nationalism was not, as alleged, a mere cloak for technical ignorance, and in course of time he gave to the world a treasury of nationalistic musical art, and an army of pupils each of whom was able to reflect no little glory upon the master to whom he owed so much.

(11)

In the hostility, to which we have referred, between two artistic camps, we have a tradition which has not yet died out in Russia. The grounds of conflict have shifted, but the strife continues.

But so long as the discussion is not confined to musicians themselves, it can do much good. So long as temperament exists there must remain a prejudice in favour of one's own temperamental outlook. Music is the language in which the message of art can be conveyed to the temperament. If, therefore, as the fruit of controversy, we succeed in inducing humanity at large to seek an acquaintance with that language, it will not matter so much that prejudice and intolerance have been so conspicuous in the attitude of the combatants who have fought against each other under the banner of art.

The opposition to the nationalist band consisted

of two united bodies and a third which was independent. " During the whole period of Glinka's activity," says Stassof,[1] " and of the first half of Dargomijsky's, there had been only two classes of musical society : the one consisting of composers, the other of public and critics. At the close of the 'fifties there appeared a new class—the musical institutions. Prior to this our musical education had been a sporadic growth . . . some of our musicians being self-taught, others having learned under the guidance of some native or foreign teacher or professor. The time had come when the need of schools, conservatoires, incorporated societies and musical denominations and prerogatives was being canvassed." Russian musicians viewed with jealous eyes the indisputable advantages possessed by the carefully educated Westerns, and sought to establish in their own land a means of obtaining a complete musical education. Unfortunately, however, while desirous of endowing Russia with a properly constituted educational body, the prime movers ignored in their haste the movement already begun by Balakiref and his disciples, and invited teachers from the principal European centres, who speedily brought into Russia not only the fruits of their experience but of their prejudices.

The first decisive step was the formation of the

[1] *Twenty-five Years of Russian Art.* V. V. Stassof.

Russian Musical Society in 1859, in which Anton Rubinstein took a leading part. Twelve months later a Moscow branch came into being at the instigation of the celebrated virtuoso's brother. This was followed in 1862 by the opening of the Petrograd Conservatoire, and in 1866 by the foundation of a similar institution in Moscow. At the head of these were respectively the two brothers, Anton and Nicholas Rubinstein. The former, prior to the initiation of this educational movement, had clearly shown his contempt for the " amateurs " of the nationalist group in a newspaper article ; this was answered by a forceful plea for freedom as well as nationalism in art, written by Stassof, who expressed himself as viewing with alarm the proposal to introduce academic ideas and stereotyped notions from abroad. In his opinion the importation of foreign grammarians could only result in the flooding of Russia with adepts having no real vocation for music.

" And then," in the words of S. N. Krouglikof,[1] himself an adherent of the " Five," " the war began." The cudgels of the nationalists were taken up and wielded with considerable effect by Cui and Stassof, the latter with a trueness of aim that was wanting from Cui's rather wild but none the less vigorous blows. The scribes of the orthodox party were Laroche, who became an

[1] Krouglikof was a pupil of Lyadof.

untiring supporter of Tchaikovsky, Solovief, who sought to execute a flank movement by complaining of Cui's conduct in military quarters, Famintsin, Theophilus Tolstoi, and others. Their portraits are to be found in Moussorgsky's scena, *The Peepshow*, which gives a highly coloured picture of their several prejudices. The crushing comments of Rubinstein, who referred to the nationalists' technical shortcomings, were parried by Cui's declaration that Rubinstein might be a Russian composer, but was not a composer of Russian music. Tchaikovsky, having coquetted with the nationalists' folk-tune principle, was charged by Balakiref with having converted his native folk-song to the Lutheran faith. The German tradition of thematic development was flouted by the " Five," and this brought down upon their heads the wrathful indignation of the conservative party. Cui's rejoinder took the form of a satirical conjecture as to whether, if one fell ill, it would not be in the very worst taste to get cured by an unorthodox method instead of dying according to the rules.

Then to these disputants there came another in the person of V. V. Serof, the " Counsellor Iserof " introduced by Wagner to Mme Judith Gauthier and Villiers de l'Isle-Adam, at Triebschen in 1858. Charged to " uphold firmly the Wagnerian standard in Petrograd," he did so with such good will that when the German composer visited the Russian capital in 1863 he received representations from certain friends of Rubinstein (one of his most implacable antagonists) asking him to intercede with Serof on behalf of the pianist whom Serof cordially hated and had bitterly attacked. The latter's position was one of isolation, and he carried on a dual warfare against the pseudo-Russians of the Conservatoire and the nationalists, having transactions with Cui and Stassof in which he fared rather badly.

(12)

In the end this bloodless battle of Petrograd concluded in a way by no means unsatisfactory to the " Five " and their camp-followers. Rimsky-Korsakof, already favourably known as a budding composer, was invited to become a member of the Conservatoire staff ; Balakiref succeeded Rubinstein as conductor of the Musical Society, seizing this golden opportunity of making known the works of his disciples ; Serof, gratified by the success of an opera in which he had sought to apply Wagnerian principles in the treatment of native folk-song, had become rather more friendly towards his old nationalist enemies. Thus it was that Petrograd became for a time identified with the nationalist group, and Moscow the stronghold

of the " occidentalists " or " eclectics," over whom
Tchaikovsky eventually presided.

With the dispersal of the original *personnel* of
the Balakiref circle, which became merged in the
early 'eighties in the group surrounding Belayef—
the famous patron and publisher—the " Young
Russian School " formulated aims a little more
liberal, and it fell to Glazounof, Belayef's first
protégé, to steer a course between the two currents
of Russian music, thus gaining the respect of both
parties.

It is Belayef whom Russia has to thank that the
somewhat academic views later formed by Glazounof have not been acquiesced in by musical society
as a whole. It says much for Belayef's enlighten-
ment and catholicity of taste that he supported
young Skryabin with no less enthusiasm than that
manifested many years earlier on behalf of Glazounof. The fruit of that championship is seen in the
present contest between the young progressives
and the older generation, in which the former
show themselves well able to hold their own.

Meanwhile, the example of Glinka and the
energies of the " Five " have been fertile.
Although the primitive nationalists' method is a
thing of the past, composers having ceased to base
their music upon folk-tunes, and operas and symphonies being no longer devoted exclusively to the
celebration of the great figures and episodes of

national and political history, musical nationalism
is by no means moribund. It is expressed rather
more subtly, and in the dramatic works of a
Stravinsky is apt to elude the foreigner. Still,
programmatic nationalism of the older type is
reflected in certain works of Prokofief, and Glazounof and Gniessin have written works in honour
of Russia's greatest poets, painters and sculptors.
And there are younger men who are rallying to
support the banner on which Moussorgsky wrote
" Towards New Territories ! "—men for whom
that motto is still pregnant with meaning, and
whose works will keep Russia's place in the front
rank of the musical nations of the world.

SKRYABIN

CHAPTER II

SKRYABIN

(1)

THE attitude of the British public towards Skryabin cannot, on the whole, be considered as having been friendly. But it would be very unfair to blame the public for that. Encouraged by concert-givers in his determination to regard the unfamiliar as a thing to be shunned, the concert-goer has developed the habit of bestowing approval only upon the established work—without any profound appreciation of its architectonic qualities or merits—and of eschewing the strange. A composer who has been fortunate enough to win the favour of the large public by means of a particularly compelling work, knows perfectly well that by this work his reputation must stand ; he will henceforth be known exclusively as the writer of a certain popular piece of music. He is not allowed to forget that if his name is to appear on a programme it must be in association with the composition that has brought him fame, and he knows that if he were to announce a programme entirely comprised of his hitherto unheard creations it would attract far less attention than a concert in which the familiar and assimilated example could be listened to.

But in Skryabin's case the circumstances were rather more disquieting. Prior to the historic repetition performance of *Prometheus* his name was unknown to the average British music-lover. By the few his career had for years been watched with an interest not diminished by his apparent affection for the idiom of Chopin. There had been a quality in his earliest creative attempts that proclaimed him to be something more than a mere imitator of his Polish idol. There was ample ground for branding him as a rather too enthusiastic worshipper ; but it was evident, at the same time, that the unfailing charm investing every page he wrote during the period of his infatuation could emanate from nowhere but his own creative nature. From the very first, too, Skryabin had shown that despite his Chopinolatry he possessed an individual habit of thought that might at some future time evolve a weighty message to musical mankind.

Fortunately for those who wished to ascertain whether that probability was in actual process of materialization, there were occasional performances of compositions bearing witness that Skryabin had no intention of limiting himself to the creation of works in which the interest of a masterly reproduction of the Chopinistic idiom was heightened by an added individual charm. The Philharmonic Society's production of the Choral Symphony and Mr. Arthur Rubinstein's performance of the fifth sonata were reassuring, particularly the latter. It was already obvious that Skryabin was beginning to find himself.

These manifestations passed unobserved, however, by the general musical public, and, for it, the first intimation of Skryabin's existence came with the performance of *Prometheus* at Queen's Hall. Rumours of the composer's revolutionary ideas had got abroad, and to such an extent was expectation aroused that, probably for the first time in musical history, an evening paper arranged to " report " the production on the day of the event itself.

The audience discovered in due course that it had not been misled, and eventually divided itself into two sections : those who claimed to be accessible to a new idea on reflection, and those who were convinced that they were not. The latter left the hall after vigorously hissing the first performance, naturally considering that to listen to the second would for them be a grievous waste of time.

(2)

While those who were more or less prepared, by a study of the composer's earlier work, for a reasoned consideration of *Prometheus*, must have been exceedingly grateful for this opportunity of observing the then more or less recent manifestation of the composer's progress, it must be reckoned that on the whole its production before a British audience was ill-timed. To offer to a public markedly averse from the contemplation of the novel,'the work of an unknown composer couched in an idiom that had set by the ears a community fully prepared for this revolt against the past, was extremely unwise, and the progress of Skryabin-culture in Britain was thereby rather impeded than assisted.

The reception of *Prometheus* by the Russian critics was not very different, in outward appearance, from that of the British. The difference consists in that the former knew that they could ill afford to be entirely flippant in dealing with the case, sorely tempted as they were thus to indulge themselves. This distinction is of the utmost importance. The newspaper-reading public is not to be misled into a complete indifference towards a revolutionary composer—provided it be clear that he is a man of established reputation—no matter how much the critic may fulminate against him. And in Russia, Skryabin's name was widely known as that of an exceptionally gifted pianist, and of a composer whose æsthetic development was not likely to be impeded by such obstacles as a misguided valuation of tradition. The Russian public, in consequence, was inclined to be sympathetic towards this daring innovator. It had already acquired some knowledge of his æsthetic ideals through acquaintance with the *Divine Poem* and the *Poem of Ecstasy*, and was not at all dismayed by the ambitious " programme " of *Prometheus*. As for the complex music, the public was apparently satisfied that an established musician might be credited with having provided something worthy of closer acquaintance, a work which, to adopt and adapt a familiar metaphor, did not wear its soul on its sleeve.

Ere long *Prometheus* attracted the attention of certain poets who took upon themselves the elucidation of its idealistic message. They and the public, having been patient towards its musical texture, are now by way of reaping a reward in the shape of aural comprehension. The labours of several disciples of the composer are beginning to bear fruit, and it is no exaggeration to say that Skryabin's output, having emerged from the condition of being the most discussed, is now the most performed music of the day.

It may be recorded that there remain a few critics who basely uphold the worst traditions of Russian musical criticism. They continue to hurl irrelevant epithets at a composer who, fortunately for himself, was not in the least affected by their strictures. The history of music is not yet long but it contains abundant warnings to such folk.

In Russia, then, Skryabin has been an institution for the past twenty years or so. From the time of his first acquaintance with the Russian Mæcenas, M. P. Belayef, and the publication of his earliest works by the firm of Jurgenson until his death, a ceaseless flow of piano pieces, punctuated by an occasional symphonic work, came from his pen.

(3)

His exceptional talent as an executant contributed also to the establishment of a world-wide reputation. His recital tours took him not only to all the most important musical centres of his native land, but also into several foreign countries, such as Germany, Holland, Belgium, France, Switzerland, the United States, and finally to Great Britain. Lastly, there is to be recorded his pedagogical activity, extending from 1897 until 1903, during which period he held a piano professorship at the Moscow Conservatoire.

In face of this record it will be recognized that if there should remain in any quarter a doubt as to Skryabin's right to be taken seriously it is time that such doubt should be dispelled. Face to face with these facts one is obliged at all events to admit that the work of a man who has entered the most important spheres of his art and has made himself felt in such a degree is not to be lightly dismissed, however unorthodox it may at first appear to be. One of the composer's biographers has devoted a number of pages to the compilation of an "historical parallel" between the contemporary verdicts pronounced on the progressive works of the greatest composers in the annals of music and of that returned against Skryabin by critics whose gaze did not penetrate quite so far into the future as his. It is extremely doubtful whether any good purpose is served by such a compilation, for it only begs the question.

The lesson that has yet to be learned by the majority of those who participate in the world's musical activities is that progress is not merely the prerogative of music, but its main function ; that it is the essential nature of music to go forward, hand in hand with social and mental evolution. The man whose obvious intention is to gaze into the future should be regarded at least as a would-be saviour, and not, at any rate, as a wilful destroyer of his art. To recall the sad errors of the Piccinists, or Artusi's indictment of the *Cruda Amarilli*, is merely to demonstrate that works of genius are often undervalued. What has yet to be widely proclaimed is that while the music of the past is entitled to our reverence because of its association with the master whose innermost feelings it expressed, the music of the future should concern us more, since it is that music which is to be associated with our immediate progeny. Napoleon's success as an " ancestor " may not have been considerable, but his pride in having recognized the importance of that estate as compared with the passive condition of descendant is one of his lovable attributes.

Let us then accord to Skryabin the moderate credit of having desired to serve his art as well as in him lay, and proceed to examine, with attention and with respect, what in him lay.

(4)

To a musician favoured by Fortune to the extent of one really musical progenitor, it must have seemed hard that he should be denied the early parental guidance that, but for an unkindly fate, he might have enjoyed.

From his mother Skryabin inherited a gift that began to manifest itself at an early age. But as she did not long survive his birth, one can only conjecture as to what her offspring might have become had his primary education been directed by so accomplished a musician as she seems to have been. It would appear to be more than probable that his youthful taste for free artistic

44

expression would not have been allowed to reflect itself in his music.

It is a little strange that there should be any doubt about the precise date of the birth of a person so recently born and so speedily famous as our subject. Yet it is only since his death that it has been established, apparently beyond doubt, that Alexander Nicholaevich Skryabin first saw the light on Christmas Day, 1871, and not, as hitherto supposed, on December 29th.

His parents had begun their short-lived matrimonial partnership when both were little more than students. The father, Alexander Ivanovich, the second of seven sons of an artillery colonel, did not graduate from Petrograd University until after the marriage, and Lioubof Petrovna, his young wife, had but recently carried off the " artist's medal " from the Conservatoire, where she had been one of Leschetitsky's most brilliant pupils. They had for some months been resident in Saratof, where the newly-fledged lawyer had established himself as an advocate, when, during a Christmas visit to his parents in Moscow, the future composer made his appearance.

Six weeks after the birth of her baby the mother was found to be in consumption. In the September following it became necessary that she should seek a warmer climate, and she went accordingly to the shores of Lake Garda. There, when her little son was hardly more than a year old, she died, and was buried.

The widower did not return to Saratof. Having specialized for a time in Oriental languages, he secured a post in the diplomatic service, finally attaining the post of Consul-General at Erzerum.

Meanwhile the little boy was being well looked after by the grandmother, in whose house he had been born. When the time arrived for his education to begin, her only daughter undertook this duty. Skryabin never forgot his indebtedness to these two good ladies.

(5)

Many evidences of his early musical capabilities are cited. If not the most important, the most startling were a wonderful ear and a phenomenal memory. When six years old he was able to play through a piece that he had just heard for the first time on a military band, and at eight he caused considerable astonishment by giving a note-perfect rendering, without the music, of a Bach gavotte and of Mendelssohn's *Gondolier's Song*, after one hearing. At this time he displayed a taste for cutting out fantastic figures in wood and for embroidery, in which pastimes he always preferred working out his own patterns. This is said to have been a characteristic trait, and one is entitled by the proverbial relationship between child and man to regard it as the germ of that later desire for self-assertion through the medium of art. " Above all," states one of his biographers, " he was an exceedingly industrious and painstaking child. It was never necessary to oblige him to work. On the contrary, he particularly disliked sitting idle."

He was already fond of poetry and the drama. In satisfaction of the latter taste he again showed a preference for his personal conceits, and we are told that when he was not the actual author of the plays " produced " in his toy theatre he chose to adapt such stories as Gogol's famous tale about the man who mislaid his nose.

Being intended for the army, the boy was placed, when ten years old, in the Moscow Cadet Corps, quickly becoming popular among his young comrades, whose attention to his piano-playing was something more than merely respectful. The interest of his masters was aroused by his good work in the entrance examination, but the promise of a zealous, and perhaps brilliant, pupil was not fulfilled. The military career failed to interest the boy. He was his mother's son, and had a ready ear for the call of music.

Its hold upon him was not at this time regarded by his family as likely to prove disastrous to the calling they had chosen for him ; but his gift was sufficiently evident for them to accede to the youngster's wish that it should be cultivated, and it was accordingly arranged that he should take lessons from G. E. Konius, the well-known composer. Later on he began a course of theoretical instruction with the man to whom he came to owe much of his subsequent contrapuntal mastery—Sergei Taneyef.

With these lessons began the transition from the military to the musical career. In 1889, young Skryabin found himself simultaneously a cadet in his final course and a candidate for the Conservatoire. For the latter estate Taneyef was no doubt responsible ; the commencing student was placed in his counterpoint class, in that of Safonof for the piano, and his taste for composition was to have been cultivated by that ephemerally famous composer, Arensky, who confessed his entire failure to discover any remarkable symptoms of such gift.

The transition period came to an end two years later, when, soon after completing his cadet course, he emerged from the Conservatoire and leaped almost immediately into fame.

(6)

It is not often that the budding musician, be he never so talented, enjoys the good fortune encountered at this time by Skryabin. Success as

SKRYABIN.

a student does not always secure an immediate acknowledgment outside the Conservatoire walls. But Russian musical society was just now enjoying the beneficence of Belayef, an enlightened and far-seeing patron of the art, and the young pianist, having been favoured with his acquaintance, speedily won his esteem. Skryabin, yesterday a student looking forward somewhat anxiously to the attainment of the first rung of the ladder of fame, found himself supported in such manner that the ascent became comparatively easy. Belayef, whose patriotic music-publishing firm had been founded a few years earlier, placed the concern at Skryabin's disposal, gave him the *entrée* to his famous Circle, began a zealous propaganda on the young composer's behalf, and arranged a recital tour of Europe.

Virtuosity had, however, no great attraction for Skryabin, and he never ceased to regard the creative side of his art as of the greater importance. Despite the trying conditions of a concert-recitalist's life, the time spent in journeying round the Continent was productive of quite a number of compositions, among which was the first sonata. He continued giving concerts, many of them in the provincial towns of Russia, where by means of his success in the dual capacity of composer and executant, and thanks to Belayef's efforts on his behalf, he had established a considerable reputation, until 1897, when, being invited to take up a professorship at the Moscow Conservatoire, he accepted this post in his *alma mater*. It was in this year that his first symphony was produced at the Russian Symphony Concerts, founded by Belayef in 1885, and that the second and third sonatas were completed.

The ensuing five years saw an ever-increasing creative activity; among the many fruits of this period were the second symphony, produced by the Moscow branch of the Imperial Russian Musical Society, under the direction of Safonof. A third symphony had already been begun, and a number of projects were forming in the composer's mind. In order to devote more time to writing, Skryabin now relinquished his post at the Conservatoire, a step which was followed by an exceedingly prolific period. In the one year he is said to have composed the fourth sonata and upwards of forty other works for the piano, among them being the *Tragic* and *Satanic* poems, and he finished also a third symphony, the *Divine Poem*.

Following this came a long sojourn abroad. Having paid visits to Geneva, Paris, where the *Divine Poem* was produced in the spring of 1905, and Genoa, he set out, towards the close of 1906, for a concert tour of the United States. Returning to Europe four months later he revisited Paris, and there took part in the festival of Russian music.

At this splendid series of concerts his second symphony and the piano concerto were performed.

His wanderings were not yet at an end, but the roving existence does not appear to have been detrimental to his creative work. During the month of January, 1908, he completed, while in Switzerland, the *Poem of Ecstasy*, begun prior to his departure for America, and composed the wonderful fifth sonata, the entire work occupying him only between three and four days.

After a brief visit to Biarritz he then settled in Brussels. Whilst in residence there he revisited his native land to take part in one of the Imperial Russian Musical Society's concerts, in the programme of which the third symphony, the *Poem of Ecstasy*, and the fifth sonata were included. It was not until the spring of 1910 that the exile, returning to his native heath, settled once again in Moscow, after an absence of just six years.

At this moment was apparently begun the friendship between Skryabin and Kussevitsky, the contrabassist turned conductor, who proved one of the composer's warmest advocates. The first demonstration of this championship was the concert tour of the Volga, upon which the two friends embarked shortly after Skryabin's return from abroad. This was the initial step in a propaganda in which Kussevitsky was hardly less successful than Belayef in his efforts on Skryabin's behalf.

123089

To him now fell the responsibility of introducing the composer's *Poem of Fire*, which had been finished during the summer of 1910.

(7)

From this time on Skryabin's reputation as an executant was quite overshadowed by the notoriety arising from the discussion of his transcendental views on his art. The circumstance that the scheme of *Prometheus* embraced a part for piano solo resulted, however, in his frequent appearance on the platform. Tours in Russia, Switzerland, Belgium, Holland and Germany accounted for a good deal of his time, but he nevertheless found leisure for composition, and two more sonatas for piano were forthcoming ere the end of 1912. By the following year the last three of his ten works in this form were complete. In the spring of 1914 he, for the first time, visited England, from whose shores he had often been but a few hours distant. His series of recitals in London, and his appearance at Queen's Hall, evoked an unusual amount of interest. That the iconoclast was no truculent Goth was manifest in the extreme delicacy of his playing, and while his curious artistic outlook was viewed with a certain uneasiness, there was entire unanimity as to his wonderful executive powers.

A return visit arranged for the following year was abandoned owing to the war, and thus Skryabin's belated first appearance in this country was unhappily his last.

The composer had nearly run the course of his earthly existence, but had by no means reached the zenith of his artistic evolution. The combined appeal of harmonic and colour blends which he had made to the senses in *Prometheus* was but a preliminary to a much wider scheme. His thoughts had for some time been busy with a work in which the emotions were to be approached through the senses by a synthetic work of art. The "Mystery," to the actual creation of which he devoted the summer of 1914, had been taking shape in his mind for many years, and its composition was occupying him at the time of his death. The text of the introductory section had been completed, and, says Gunst, "he had begun to compose the music, which he had hoped to finish by the autumn of 1915, but fate willed otherwise . . ."

During his stay in London he had suffered a good deal of pain from a tumour in the upper lip, which subsequently developed into a carbuncle. All the efforts of the doctors in attendance were in vain, and on April 14th, 1915, Skryabin breathed his last.

53

(8)

In the composer of *Prometheus* we have a progressive artist who, impelled by the conviction that art was both a medium of self-expression and a means of human intercourse, proposed to extend its boundaries in three entirely different and immensely important directions.

In the first place there is what may be termed the purely physical direction, namely, the introduction of a scale which had not hitherto been associated with art-music. This reconstruction or reconstitution was, of course, intended to provide a more flexible instrument of expression.

The second innovation with which we may credit (or tax) him is that of making an appeal simultaneously to the eye and the ear. In this region we have not yet been able to follow his experiment, since no performance of the *Poem of Fire* has yet taken place in England in which the colour instrument has figured, but we are able to understand that such an alliance of sound and colour would considerably increase the social power of an art-work. Thirdly, there is the definite association of abstract (as apart from dramatic or devotional) music with a spiritual idea and creed.

Of these three innovations the first has perhaps caused the least concern among those who are intolerant of artistic experiment. This comparative

54

indifference (it may be described as indifference when compared with the consternation aroused by the other items of Skryabin's agenda) was no doubt due to the spade-work of Debussy, whose tonal scale has borne the brunt of an opposition that would otherwise have exerted its full force against Skryabin and his harmonic scale, or, for the matter of that, any other attempt or proposal to oust the approved system of harmony from an undisputed sovereignty.

It is questionable whether the harmonic scale system can be expected to serve satisfactorily as a medium for a multitude of composers. Its very origin argues against that supposition. The question as to whether Skryabin first evolved the system or the harmony that is spoken of as its derivative is apparently answered by the appearance in the Valse, Opus 1, of a harmony which may be considered as a hint of things that were to come. On this evidence one feels justified in believing that the evolution of the harmonic scale, as used by Skryabin, which may be briefly described as consisting of six notes drawn from the series of overtones (beginning with the seventh) : C, D, E, F sharp, A, B flat, and their disposition in fourths, must have been brought about by the anxiety of a trained musician to set his house in order—to erect a system around a spontaneous idea in order to maintain a link between a well-defined past and a nebulous future. Certain recognizable features of the chord, which is supposed to characterize the essentials of Skryabin's mysticism, being observable in the early works of the first period, one is justified in assuming that Skryabin first discovered his partiality for this chord, and afterwards evolved the system by which it is embraced. In any case we may decide that an arbitrary choice of a medium such as this cannot be considered a satisfactory method of seeking a new means of expressing human emotions.

The fascinating problem as to whether the mental or sensorial susceptibilities to a correspondence between colours and sounds will ever be sufficiently developed to give to an art in which they are combined what Rimsky-Korsakof—who, like many another musician, was deeply interested in the question—termed " rights of citizenship," has been the subject of a number of essays in a variety of tongues. The experiments made with Professor Rimington's colour-organ and Skryabin's *tastiera per luce*, or " keyboard of light," do not appear to have favourably impressed those present.

But it does not seem unlikely that, in course of time, we may evolve a colour-language that will roughly correspond with the musical language of society, which is after all only half conventionalized at the present time ; beyond labelling certain music as definitely sad or joyful in character, we should hardly care to commit ourselves to any comprehensive musical vocabulary of the emotions. And it should not be forgotten that we cannot decide upon the efficacy of the correspondence until we are able to satisfy ourselves that the composer's colour-stave has been correctly interpreted on the keyboard of light. A bad performance has often been the cause of an erroneous estimate of a novel work.

As to the association of music with a spiritual idea, it should not be imagined that Skryabin's music celebrates the Deity in musico-theosophical terms. It has a rather narrower significance in one way, an even broader in another. Skryabin is celebrating himself as the central figure around which the process of evolution is being carried out. He describes that process in theosophical terms because they are best fitted, in his view, for the expression of that idea. But it is the universal human privilege of self-realization and the power of self-affirmation which Skryabin set himself to reveal ; and his proclamation of the universality of the creative power, the gift of Prometheus, is but the reiteration of an eternal truth. The association of Skryabin's spiritual message with a particular sect is thus an idea which it would be best altogether to dismiss.

(9)

If it is to his symphonic works that one must go for a franker statement of Skryabin's spiritual message, we are granted an adequate insight into his purely musical or harmonic development by the easier means of a perusal of his piano works, which afford also a fairly clear indication of the composer's psychological evolution. The ten sonatas give an approximately definite sketch-plan of his progress, which may be filled in by reference to his many pieces in the smaller forms. " They," says Gunst, " are a corner stone on which he erects storey by storey an edifice that reaches to the height of the monuments left by the classic masters."

Skryabin's musical life may be roughly divided into four periods. At the outset he was a passionate lover of Chopin, and, on his own confession, often, when a youngster, slept with a volume of the Polish master's works beneath his pillow. The conclusion of this phase is marked by the third sonata, which was composed before any orchestral example had appeared, and in which, according to Skryabin, may be found the last examples of his Chopinistic manner. The next period brought the composer under various other influences, notably those of Wagner and Liszt, and, on occasion, that of Tchaikovsky. The first symphony

(Opus 26) shows that the old allegiance has not yet been thrown off ; but in the fourth sonata it is clearly to be seen that the " Ego," to which Skryabin was striving to give freedom, is about to express itself. The idea of the dignity of creation clearly enters into its psychological programme. This, perhaps the most fruitful period, includes the *Divine Poem* for orchestra, the eight Preludes (Opus 42), and the *Tragic* and *Satanic* poems for piano.

The remarkable fifth sonata is sometimes considered as closing the second period ; but whilst it may be regarded as a culminating point in the evolution of the composer's psychological and harmonic individuality, to which the first symphony and the *Divine Poem* lead up, it represents so definite a break with the fettered past, and is so closely allied to the later sonatas in respect of its underlying idealogy, as to merit a place in the third, or completely individual period, in which it would rank as a preliminary manifestation of that apotheosis of individualism mooted in the *Poem of Ecstasy*, and finally reached in *Prometheus*.

In the fourth and final period Skryabin made such a rapid advance as to draw his music beyond the comprehension of most of his contemporaries and even of some of his warmest advocates. The new harmonic system, which receives a tolerably simple exposition in the *Poem of Fire*, is given a fuller sway in the seventh sonata, already fore-shadowed in the smaller framework of *Etrangeté* (Opus 63). The three studies (Opus 65), written in ninths, sevenths and fifths respectively, must of course be considered apart, as conforming in matter to the signification of their generic title ; but the third is noticeably less complex, so far as concerns the ear, than its fellow studies, and not more so than the works which fell between this series and *Prometheus*. The *Prelude* (No. 2, Opus 67), the *Poem* (No. 1, Opus 69), and the very charming second number of the same set may be cited as examples that do not require quite so close an application on the part of those who seek to appreciate their inner beauty. For the bolder spirits the first of the two dances (Opus 73) may be recommended as constituting a milestone in the composer's harmonic evolution ; while an appetite for strangeness should be appeased by a perusal of the first of the five *Preludes* (Opus 74), in which set, however, No. 2 forms a conspicuous exception to the general obscurity.

(10)

The Chopinistic manner of Skryabin is a musical phenomenon not easily reducible to a verbal description. Skryabin, although idolizing the master, never rendered him the doubtful service of deliberate imitation. To be assured of this, one does not need a declaration from the Muscovite composer. His early works do not resemble the model as do the Mozartean experiments of Tchaikovsky and Rimsky-Korsakof. The resemblance is more or less of a spiritual nature. Consideration of the physical resemblance recalls the British painter, James Clark Hook, whose pictures usually took the form of land or seascapes, but whose almost invariable practice of placing a figure or two in the foreground earned for his productions the description of "Hookscapes." Some of the early works of Skryabin appear at a distance to lack any evidence of individuality, but as we draw closer to them we perceive, on many occasions, an harmonic feature that proclaims the music to be that of a composer who has either insufficient self-discipline, or too much individuality, to imitate successfully.

This applies principally to the earliest pieces. Curiously enough, in the second phase of the first period, this embryo of musical individuality is by no means conspicuous, and thus, when we reach the *Concert-Allegro* (Opus 18), the third bar of which contains a harmony that is completely characteristic, we might easily have forgotten that we were dealing with the work of a man who, at the outset, appeared to have a message of his own to deliver. Only one of the intervening numbers can be held to constitute a reminder. The five *Preludes* (Opus 16)—with the exception of the charming little miniature, No. 4—while giving no harmonic foretaste of the later Skryabin, have very little spiritual affinity with Chopin's music.

Following the *Concert-Allegro* we have ample signs of the awakening individuality, which continues to assert itself with increasing force until the *Preludes* (Opus 35), in which there is a recrudescence of Chopinism (in No. 1) combined with other foreign influences—those of Wagner and Schumann—in the second and third. These are evidences of a passing eclecticism to which we owe the character of the *Satanic Poem*, whose characteristic chord of the ninth with augmented fifth does little to dispel the general Lisztian flavour of the work.

Noticeable, not only in the early works but in all Skryabin's compositions of the smaller kind, is a wonderful appropriateness of title when any such poetic indication occurs, a remarkable unity of style in the connected pieces under such generic headings as " Preludes " and " Etudes," and a happy gift displayed in an appropriate choice of key. In this last quality we have a resemblance between the endowments of Chopin and Skryabin that is seemingly unimportant. It gains in significance as soon as we become aware that the two composers had key-tastes very much in common, and especially in view of Skryabin's association of colour with sound. One imagines that a composer who had given so much attention to this question would be more inclined than another to ponder his choice of key. And yet the unfailing " rightness " in the selection of tonality leads one to the conviction that such choice was altogether spontaneous.

As a refutation of some hasty verdicts that have credited Skryabin with a sudden departure from every harmonic and formalistic precedent, the sonatas are as complete a document as could well be desired. They form a progression so nicely graded as completely to dispel any such illusion. And it is not only the harmonic evolution that is so plainly marked out in these works, for the gradual withdrawal from the vexatious limitations imposed by consideration of formalistic tradition is no less clearly to be traced. Furthermore, they constitute a more accessible guide to the composer's spiritual development than the symphonies, and if this does not help us to comprehend the physical qualities of his music it lends an added interest.

(11)

The Chopinist influence, chief among those easily determined, is of course paramount in the first sonata (Opus 6), and beyond certain vague suggestions both in the harmonic and the melodic content this work shows little that can be characterized as an individual utterance of the composer.

The advance shown in the *Sonata-Fantasia* (Opus 19) in G sharp minor, is manifested more by the wonderful manipulation of the thematic substance than by any particular novelty of matter or manner. This example was completed only after five years had elapsed since its inception ; the final *Presto* appears to be the fruit of the last period of labour on the work, and its thematic contour has much in common with Skryabin's later melodic manner.

The third sonata was begun in the year in which its forerunner was completed. In this, altogether apart from considerations of form and harmony, we have to deal with a step forward in respect of the avowed poetic or psychological basis which we are now accustomed to seek in Skryabin's larger works. Its mystical presentment of the struggles of the soul is of course the herald of the idealogy of the *Divine Poem*, the *Poem of Ecstasy* and *Prometheus*. Together with this development we observe, in the third sonata, the exploitation of the chord which called for the search for a new harmonic system. Here, as in the second symphony (Opus 29), we find this chord in the embryonic shape of augmented ninth and sharpened fifth. With the piano *Poem* (Opus 32) the third symphony (*Divine Poem*), Opus 43, we discover it in its fuller form. Of this work there exists a " programme," not written but sanctioned by the composer. It is entitled " Soul-states." The soul of man, not yet strong enough to resist " allurements " and " vague desires," and having made a valiant effort, " falls overwhelmed into the abyss of nothingness."

Skryabin's sonatas up to the fourth are divided into movements entirely separate from each other. The two movements of this work are numbered, but are in reality an Introduction (Andante) and a main movement, joined to the introductory matter, moreover, by the connecting word " *attacca*." Henceforth the sonatas were to take the form of " Poems," without break of any kind. The fourth sonata shows also an increase in evidences of an idealistic " programme." Even without knowledge of the literary foundation of the preceding sonata, one could hardly fail to notice that in the character of the themes there is a distinct indication that the music is not " absolute " in the completest sense of that term. It is a little odd that, in the circumstances, Skryabin has not here found it necessary to inaugurate his later procedure of giving profuse interpretatory counsels, such as those in the later works and in examples of the *Etude* class. One understands, however, that the first theme is the

" motive of desire," and the second that of " anguish."

In the fourth sonata we have observed symptoms of a coming change in form. In the fifth (Opus 53) the change is complete. The harmonic progress is marked, and the mystical " programme " is announced by means of a quotation from the text of the *Poem of Ecstasy* which was written just before. This avowal of a psychological foundation to the music is accompanied by the appearance of expression notes that are more descriptive than conventional. The chords which follow a sinister downward leap are, it is intimated, to be played " sotto voce misterioso affanato," while the imperious response a few bars later is to be given with no uncertain emphasis " quasi trombe."

A further step towards freedom is taken in the sixth sonata, in which the composer discards the key-signature as a device no longer of practical benefit to him. He has already, we may be sure, felt its irksomeness when penning the development section of the preceding sonata, in which there is a succession of key changes symbolizing, as in *Prometheus*, the process of evolution and involution. There is also to be remarked, in the recapitulation of this work, the composer's need of a third stave in order to give the three themes, here stated in juxtaposition, a visible token of a desire for independence. The chord construction differs little here from that of *Prometheus*, and the statement of harmonies on a basis of fourths is a noticeable feature.

It was with the publication of his seventh example that Skryabin, in the words of one of his disciples, " drew his music beyond the comprehension not only of the public but of the musicians." " One requires," says another writer, " not merely a huge and many-sided artistic gift in the province of the pianistic art, but a particular and profound insight into the style of Skryabin to do justice to the composer's works. One needs, in fact, to be a ' Skryabinist.' " Mention of the necessity of attaining this condition is perhaps the more appropriate at this point since this work was the composer's favourite, and was, in his estimation, "nearest in content to the ' Mystery.' " The literary content follows more or less the same line as that previously taken, but here the soul meets with " harshness " and " cruelty," and the culminating ecstasy, or orgiastic dance, is stated in musical figures that resemble the expression of a similar mood in the fifth sonata.

The same figure appears in the next sonata (Opus 66), and recurs during the course of this, the longest work of the composer in that form. Skryabin develops the principle, introduced in the fourth and repeated in the two following sonatas, of beginning with an introductory

" motto " section, opening in this instance, not as in the fifth, with a sort of " Prologue," but with the three fundamental themes themselves. The harmonic structure may be codified as deriving from the initial chord, but the musical interest, consisting also in a wealth of contrapuntal device, has now a stronger rival in the literary message, which is given an increased articulateness.

In the comparatively slight work No. 9, the plan of opening with an immediate revelation of the thematic basis of the work is retained. The economy is not only in respect of length, the structure being of altogether smaller dimensions. The composer is content with thematic and rhythmic transformations and contrapuntal interests, and there is nothing approaching the harmonic exuberance that was displayed in the twenty-five note chord used by Skryabin in the climax of the delirious frenzy of the seventh sonata.

Like the third, sixth and seventh, the ninth sonata includes in its programme the contemplation of the effect on the soul of evil influences such as are present in the *Satanic Poem*. The final sonata, in contradistinction, appears to depict a free flight unopposed by any malignant power. Towards the end the ecstatic nature of the music gives place to a calm even greater than that of the sober introduction.

For the present it were better not to approach
the later sonatas of Skryabin as separate pieces of
music, for even in the comparative simplicity of
the last two examples, in which the composer has
dispensed with everything unessential, there is
still much that is not easily to be assimilated. But
as a decalogue, in which the development of the
composer's musical individuality and his spiritual
evolution may be traced page by page, they form
a document of the utmost value.

(12)

" The symphonic works of Skryabin," writes
Saminsky, in an essay on the composer's orchestral
language, " are to be regarded as the organ of his
spiritual message " ; and one has indeed to give
but the slightest attention to these works to perceive that they are intended to fulfil a highly
significant exegetical purpose. The *Rêverie* (Opus
24) alone remains outside this classification and is
to be considered as a tentative effort in the domain
of the orchestra, having primarily a poetic, rather
than a spiritual significance. This first attempt
marks, nevertheless, an important epoch, not only
in the composer's musical life as a whole, but in
the development of that special medium through
which he chose eventually to reveal his spiritual
outlook, for it was by means of this small

symphonic essay that he came to perceive the fitness of the orchestra as an instrument on which his message could be articulated.

With the composition of the first symphony he began that series of orchestral works which are perhaps best to be described as chapters of an impersonal or objective autobiography. Properly to understand the composer's aim, however, it is necessary to bear in mind the unfinished work, towards the perfection of which Skryabin was constantly aiming during the last fifteen years or so of his life.

The " Mystery," of which only more or less rough sketches were completed, was to have been a work in which the composer's spiritual thoughts could be expressed, but in it he desired also to create an actual spiritual effect upon those before whom it was performed. In the " Mystery " he intended to embody his message in what for the sake of convenience we may call a " score," but it was to have been delivered in the form of a service that would consist of a combined and simultaneous appeal to all the senses by all the arts. The composer's avowal that " the day on which my ' Mystery ' is produced will be the happiest of my life " seems a peculiarly worldly expression in relation to such a matter as this ; the contemplation of the possibilities of such a performance as he had in mind might well lead one to the conviction that the evil spirits, to which the composer from time to time refers in his later compositions, must have begun to walk in awe of this mortal, and to them, fearful of exorcization, we must attribute the dissolution that prevented the completion of this highly spiritual design. But Skryabin's rapturous glance towards that future attainment helps us, at any rate, to perceive and to remember the relation to it of all his large symphonic works beginning with the first symphony. From the time that he first conceived the idea of the " Mystery " he bore it constantly in mind when composing his orchestral works ; his sonatas and even his smaller pieces are influenced by the thoughts evoked by its contemplation.

(13)

It is no doubt because the first symphony contains the germ of the " Mystery," that Skryabin, who looked upon it as a kind of artistic first-born, confessed to a special affection for the work. This can hardly have been engendered by the harmonic and stylistic aspect of the composition, for the composer plainly reveals in it a number of foreign influences, which are not to be regarded as contributing to the exaltation of that " Divine I " of his dreams. It is not in the music

71

of this symphony that the germ lies, but in the text of its last and choral movement, in which a chorus is introduced for the purpose of rendering a tonal apotheosis of art. The hymn to art is not, in any beyond the purely technical sense, a parallel to Beethoven's choral ode; it is the first chapter in the unfinished volume of Skryabin's spiritual and artistic self-revelation.

From what has been termed the "orpheism" of this Dædalian symphony, Skryabin proceeded to the composition of a work in which the programmatic idea of "divine play" is a special feature. In the second symphony we are asked to contemplate the soul emancipating itself from the bondage of dependence; freedom is won by the creative act, ceaselessly performed but "aimlessly," without motive. To strive without attaining, even to welcome obstacles, this is "divine play." As well as that of the soul there is the divine play of the universe: the continual process of involution and evolution, materialization and dematerialization is the "world-symphony" of universal "divine play." These expressions, which approximate to the terminology of theosophical belief, represent a temporary interest in this form of religious manifestation, from which Skryabin emerged with a broader scheme of his own contriving. Even if we agree with Engel that the second symphony is but a preparation for the

Divine Poem—the fruit of an intermediate period —we are bound to acknowledge the happiness with which the literary idea is expressed in it. The motive of " ceaseless striving " in the Allegro movement is particularly well chosen, and the manner in which it is handled in the development shows that in Skryabin, at this stage, we have a nicely balanced combination of the artist and craftsman.

But it is in the third symphony that the composer arrives both at something like a free expression of his spiritual individuality and a personal method of musical statement. Its harmonic content reveals a decided freedom from alien influences, an emancipation that was to be secured in the *Poem of Ecstasy* and ratified in *Prometheus*. There is a hint of " programme " in the titles of the three movements—the words " *Luttes*," " *Voluptés*," and " *Jeu divin* " giving us definitely to understand that the music is a record of psychological movement. The first theme irresistibly recalls that of " ceaseless striving " in the preceding symphony, but here there is an opposing force that would seek to prevent a free activity. For a time the human soul, as depicted in " *Voluptés*," is hypnotized by the allurements of sensuous pleasures, but eventually, with the awakening of a dormant intellect, the creative instinct gains the upper hand, and the soul, becoming conscious of

73

an affinity with the spirit of universal creation, attains to the kingdom of " divine play."

(14)

In the *Poem of Ecstasy* the idea of the divine play of the soul reaches its apogee, and the musical language, in which the portrayal of the spiritual movement of the soul is rendered, has become a completely individual expression.

Hitherto, beyond the text of the first symphony's hymn, the descriptive titles of the *Divine Poem* and the wealth of interpretatory notes such as " *de plus en plus triomphant,*" " *profondement tragique* " and " *élan sublime,*" there has been no programme definitely attached to any of Skryabin's orchestral works. For the *Poem of Ecstasy,* however, the composer took, as foundation, his own literary work of that name, from which is quoted the motto of the fifth sonata. The content of the literary poem is followed more or less closely by the musical. It aids us in our contemplation of the soul's struggle to obtain entrance into a state of energy describable as an orgy of creative activity. The soul, in an ecstasy, scorns achievement and rushes on towards the undertaking of further and mightier tasks. The soul here represents, we are told, the personal element evolving itself from the cosmic chaos that is again to be pictured in the

74

opening of *Prometheus*. The experiences through which it has to pass are almost meticulously described in the score of the *Poem*, but the musical language, though sufficiently individual as to be recognizable as the composer's, " even," in the words of a Russian critic, " by those not experienced in music," is sufficiently unusual to require considerable patience on the part of those who are.

It is not, however, in the *Poem of Ecstasy* that Skryabin reaches the point at which his music definitely breaks with the approved triad formation of chords. There are pages in the work which foretell the coming rupture, but the *Poem* is really nearer on its psychological side to the attainment of that spirituality to which the composer aspired in the " Mystery," than on the musical. Skryabin has found the " Divine I," but he communicates the discovery in accents a little halting, and we hardly believe him.

(15)

With *Prometheus* the musical language, if not perfected, has at least a complete vocabulary. The composer has succeeded in fully comprehending his own psychological system, and has now at his disposal the medium through which it may be expounded. The nature of the work, as originally conceived, will be understood when it is explained that according to Skryabin's intention, *Prometheus* was to take the form of a theurgical or mystical ceremony, his chorus were to be clothed in white vestments and the whole performance was to be conducted on the lines rather of a service than of a concert. Rendered in this manner, with the inclusion of the part for the " keyboard of light," it is of course a work which would have well prepared us for the " Mystery." A concert performance without the light effects reduces the work to the level of ordinary music and leaves for our consideration little more than the question of its harmonic strangeness.

As has already been said, this strangeness exists only for those who come to the contemplation of the work unprepared by acquaintance with the logical steps leading to the harmonies of *Prometheus*. And, indeed, the knowledge of Skryabin's earlier works brings with it a two-fold realization of their essential characteristics. " When we listen to *Prometheus*," says Sabaneyef, " we are able to realize that what we have lightly dismissed as purely Chopinistic is far from being such." With a knowledge of his later works the germ of Skryabin's musical individuality becomes visible from the very outset. And while his aristocratic refinement constitutes a resemblance to Chopin, his desire to address the multitude and the nature of his intended discourse give him a figure altogether titanic. Yet in these two widely different aspects of the man there is nothing incongruous. His conception of the artistic function was an exceedingly lofty one. In the ideal artist he saw the Superman whose mission it was to stimulate the sense for beauty, not only in the susceptible, but in every man. One can hardly doubt but that the " Mystery " would have been an immense revelation. The thought of it suggests the possibility of a spiritual revival brought about by means that would be compelling alike to the artist and the common man. That such a force could be set in motion by human agency seems to conflict with our conception of the limited prerogative of mortals. And we are now aware that the gods had planned otherwise. . . .

GLAZOUNOF

CHAPTER III

(1)

THE determination of Glazounof's place in the contemporary musical world presents no great difficulties. Among those creative musicians who attain distinction there are always to be found a certain number of men whose mission in art appears to be that of improving the means with a view to the perfection of the end, and in these composers we usually find an inclination to revise, purify or refine, rather than to discard the approved paraphernalia of musical creation.

When we seek for the cause of this attitude towards the musical art we often discover it in a perfect contentment with life as it has been experienced by such a composer. He has no reason to quarrel with the conditions of his environment, and he does not therefore require to use his art as a medium of vehement expression. For him, art is self-sufficing. In the creative product of such musicians we look neither for the psychological torments recorded in the pages of a Tchaikovsky score, nor for the more objective utterances which are the expression of Moussorgskian pessimism.

G 81

He is concerned with art as beauty, with music as beautiful sound. Forms are enlarged or modified not at the dictates of poetic or emotional content, but in order to cultivate formal beauty. The poetic element in music lies in its own inherent poetry. And if, on occasion, it is linked with life, and is given that literary significance that a title seems to bring into it, we find that it has not been called upon to describe the objects or occurrences at which the title hints, but merely to reflect the mood which has been engendered by the contemplation of such objects and occurrences.

For such a creative mind the principal preoccupation is the reflection of abstract beauty in abstract art. The composer, if not entirely confining himself to it, has a very decided preference for " absolute " music. His " programme " is beauty, and in most cases happiness is its inspiration.

(2)

No sooner do we begin to seek, in the circumstances of his life, for a cause of that optimistic manner of expression by which Glazounof's music is pervaded, than we are confronted with abundant evidence to account for its presence. His life has been lived in an environment of calm and refinement, and uninterrupted prosperity.

Glazounof

Belonging to a family long established in one of the most dignified of commercial pursuits, he was brought up in surroundings that differ from those of an ancient aristocratic family only in that the qualities that won the distinction conferred were still to be observed in the daily pursuit of affairs. In his family the inheritance of virtue was regarded as no less a benefit than the inheritance of distinction.

When he reached his musical majority, and his creative impulse was awakened, Glazounof had no battles to fight on behalf of his creations. Sponsors, both for performance and for publication, were found immediately. Finally, when his talents were ripened by experience and his wide knowledge of musical literature and extensive practice of composition seemed to fit him for the position of musical friend, philosopher and guide to the Russian nation, the post of Director of Petrograd Conservatoire was offered him, in circumstances so exceptional that one cannot help fancying the episode to have been arranged by the Fates—anxious that everything in this well-ordered life should be perfectly managed.

Thus Glazounof has experienced neither financial embarrassment, social isolation, nor artistic antagonism.

We are informed by his biographer that he lives in the house of his fathers, sleeps in the bed on which he was born, works in the room in which it formerly stood.

External circumstances appear to justify our styling him the Mendelssohn of Russian music.

He has been called a musical Janus, who contrives to face both the past and the future of his art. This description, applied some years ago, does not now so well fit the man whom it was intended to describe.

(3)

There is a condition of music that is never changed, and that is its changeability. In every generation the writers about music inform us, as though to quiet our forebodings, that music is clearly at this moment in a state of transition. There are few Januses in the world of music. There are those who, in the words of H. G. Wells, walk backwards into the future ; they, no doubt, are the prototypes of the folk who belong to the first of the classes into which the Russian composer and meditative essayist, Gniessin, divides all musicians confronted with innovations : some, he observes, attempt to reconcile the new with the old ; others, the old with the new. Of late years the Director of Petrograd Conservatoire has clearly indicated that he has no desire to reconcile the works of the rising Russian generation with those of the masters whom he loves so well and emulates so splendidly.

If we call him the Mendelssohn of Russian music we must hasten to remove the impression that, in our opinion, his music is superficial. It is, on the contrary, of such a nature as to suggest a long life, if not immortality. His reverence for classical forms has not blinded him to the possibilities of improving and extending the architectonic material of the past. He has certainly not left music where he found it. If, in relation to biographical matters, he is to be called the Mendelssohn of Russian music, we may style him, in so far as concerns the essentials of his art, the Brahms.

(4)

Alexander Constantinovich Glazounof was born on July 29th, 1865, at Petrograd, where his father carried on the bookselling and publishing concern originally established in Moscow in the eighteenth century. Unlike the majority of musicians who have achieved world-wide repute, Glazounof did not, in his earliest years, exhibit any signs of remarkable musical gifts. As a small boy he is said to have displayed a taste for pictures, and was happiest when copying the designs of playing-cards. It was not until a beginning had been

made with his musical instruction that he began
to show a preference for pictures with musical
subjects, particularly for those in which were to
be found the figures of players upon wind instruments "with puffed-out cheeks." "He had,"
says Ossovsky, " a great respect for the images of
conductors holding the magic baton in uplifted
hand." In these predilections, needless to say, is
discovered a hint of Glazounof's later preference
for the orchestra and for instrumental music as
a whole.

But if the usual signs of musical precocity were
at first absent, the youngster's dormant musical
tastes were assured of development on the best
possible lines as soon as they should awaken. His
mother was a talented pianist and a cultured
musician, who enjoyed the friendship of Balakiref; the boy's musical studies, therefore, were
naturally begun and proceeded with on the same
sound principles as his general education.

His first teacher, with whom he began at the
age of nine, was a lady who was able to pride
herself upon being a pupil of a then eminent
pianist, Anton Kontsky. After about two years'
instruction from her, the boy passed into the care
of Narcisse Elenkovsky, a virtuoso who, owing to
an injury to his hand, had been obliged to abandon
the platform and devote himself to teaching.
Under his guidance the young Glazounof began to

display some astonishing musical gifts and to develop a considerable taste for composition. But the sudden departure of Elenkovsky from the capital necessitated a change of teacher, and it was thus that the " little Glinka," as he was then affectionately called, came under the direct and benign influence of Rimsky-Korsakof, with whom for a little time past his mother had been taking lessons. At this moment begins the second epoch in this career of facile success. A most interesting account of Korsakof's first acquaintance with the lad is to be found in the former's Memoirs, in which the writer observes that, after a comparatively short time, the relationship of master and pupil became altered to that of mutual friendship and esteem.

There followed a rapid acquisition of technical proficiency, and, before long, Glazounof was able to produce proofs of his creative prowess—bringing to one of his lessons (in 1881) a sketch for a symphony. Ere the year was out the work had been completed, and on March 17th, 1882, Glazounof's first symphony in E minor was performed, under Balakiref's direction, at a concert of the Free School of Music. The audience, impressed with the dignity of the work, showed no little astonishment, relates Rimsky-Korsakof, when in response to a demand for the composer there came forward a youth of sixteen, attired in the uniform of a student. It was even hinted that the symphony was in reality the work of Rimsky-Korsakof, who had been commissioned by indulgent parents to lend his gifts in order to secure an easy triumph for a pampered child !

But his closest musical friends were fully convinced of the young fellow's unusual talent, and the Circle of which Rimsky-Korsakof was then the centre, and to which at this time belonged such eminent personages as Borodin, Lyadof and Stassof, the art-critic, was thrown open to him. It may be mentioned that Glazounof showed no disposition to fling himself headlong into the stream of Nationalism in music, but, while sympathizing with the Circle's aspirations, preserved his independence. By good fortune he was able a little later to confer a great benefit on the Circle and indirectly to contribute to an immense improvement in the condition of Russian music.

(5)

The circumstance here referred to is Glazounof's acquaintance with Belayef, perhaps the wisest patron in the annals of music, whose esteem for the young composer gave rise first to a desire to publish his works, and eventually, to a determination to found a publishing firm in the interests of native composers.

Glazounof

From this time on Glazounof's reputation steadily grew, not only in Russia, but in the West. Thanks to Borodin, whose transactions with Liszt are ancient history, the great Hungarian—always a firm friend of the New Russian School—conducted a vigorous propaganda on the young man's behalf; hence the performance of the first symphony at Weimar in 1884. The appearance of *Stenka Razin* and the second symphony in the programme of the Russian concerts held at the Paris Exhibition of 1889 is, of course, attributable to the enterprise of Belayef, who financed these concerts. An idea as to the rapidity with which Glazounof's reputation was now spreading may be gathered from the fact of his having been invited in 1882 to write a *pièce d'occasion* for the Chicago Columbian Exhibition—at a date only a year later than Tchaikovsky's tour of the United States. His works were soon being performed on all sides, in France, Germany and England, and in these countries as well as in his native land honours began to shower upon him. One which must have been exceptionally congenial was the invitation in 1900 to join the staff of the Petrograd Conservatoire as professor of instrumentation and score-reading. Only five years later came the crowning distinction, blown by the ill-wind which drove Rimsky-Korsakof from the post of Director of that institution, which Glazounof has since held.

Glazounof has contributed to every department of musical creation excepting Opera. At the present moment he has eight symphonies to his credit, in addition to several symphonic pieces and suites. Although he has, as yet, written no opera, he has made several essays in dramatic music—the ballets *Raymonda, Ruses of Love* and *The Seasons* are established favourites—and not the least important contribution to the theatre is his incidental music to the late Grand Duke Constantine's drama, *The King of the Jews*. His vocal works include few solo songs, but six choral compositions are to be mentioned in this category. What endears him, however, to the music-loving world as a whole—perhaps more than the symphonic works—are the charming examples for string quartet, which are among the most cherished possessions of devotees of chamber-music.

(6)

It was formerly the custom of chroniclers to refer to Glazounof as standing midway between the Nationalist and "Occidentalist" groups. That plan is not now to be commended, since it is no longer suitable ; it is out of date. There is no Nationalist group, and the composers associated by considerations of locality with the once clearly defined Moscow tradition, have such a variety of

GLAZOUNOF.

From a drawing by Serof.

styles that they cannot by any stretch of imagination be considered as constituting a group. But
if the ground on which Glazounof stands has
altered its formation, the particular spot occupied
by him remains unchanged. Surveying the field
of Russian music, he has in recent years seen
around him, each striving for an individualistic
ideal, the figures of such as Skryabin, Stravinsky,
Taneyef, Rebikof, Prokofief and Myaskovsky. The
links connecting these composers with the groups
that formerly had their homes in the ancient and
modern capitals are more or less slender, and as
frail, in some cases, as the thread connecting such
composers' products with the art of the past. One
thinks of this young and heterogeneous " school "
as a number of trees, each, after its own fashion,
representing an ideal. And among them towers
Glazounof, rooted deep in the soil of music, and
spreading his branches in almost every direction.
And the more shade he brings upon the field the
more the younger growths lean away from the
shade, stretching eagerly towards the light that
gives them life.

In adopting the arboreal metaphor, we naturally
think of the main branches as symbols of the
various musical directions in which Glazounof has
been active. We observe that he has entered every
domain of his art, other than the operatic, and
even in this sphere, which he has neglected, we are

his debtors in respect of the completion of one of
the most splendid examples of the Russian musico-
dramatic repertoire ; but for him *Prince Igor*
would not be quite so glorious a monument as it
is to Borodin.

The eight symphonies are indeed a generous
contribution to a store that not long since had no
existence. Of the symphonic suites and smaller
orchestral works, the *Middle Ages*, *The Forest*,
The Sea and *The Kremlin* carry on the tradition
that has become firmly rooted in Russian music
since first planted there by Glinka and intensively
cultivated by Liszt.

His ballets, *Raymonda* and *The Seasons*, perform
the dual service of bringing him into closer association with the younger schools and of forcing him,
as it were, to write in a more particularly descriptive manner than is his wont in his purely symphonic creations. The string quartets, quintet
and suites are by way of taking the place, once
occupied by those of Tchaikovsky, as the mainstay
of the Russian chamber-music literature.

A fine and decidedly popular violin concerto
and two piano sonatas and the " Sasha " suite
represent him in solo instrumental music, and the
score of the above-mentioned *King of the Jews*
contains examples which add lustre to his choral
work. In the region of song he has not been very
productive, and the more recent numbers show

a decrease in interest ; it is in this sphere alone that he may be said to have given little of permanent value.

Glazounof is then to be reckoned as representing the orthodox in music ; but he represents orthodoxy in many phases. In his first orchestral overture, based on Greek themes, the " little Glinka " has followed his precursor in employing crude folk-song as symphonic thematic material. *Stenka Razin* pays a tribute to the musico-historical method of nationalism, and *The Forest* and *The Kremlin* to a more abstract type of programmatic creation. The later symphonies have shown that he can write music that, far from being less interesting than his programmatic works, have a strength and beauty that have yet to be estimated at their true value as examples of Russian music.

As to the chamber works, they are, in some instances, purely classical in form ; but no one acquainted with the *Novelettes*, for string quartet, can fail to see in them the influence of Belayef's festive gatherings.

(7)

In an exceedingly interesting disquisition upon the question of Glazounof's fidelity to the orchestra, the Russian critic Ossovsky declares that the composer's comparative neglect of the forms in which the voice predominates is not to be attributed so much to personal inclination as to the influence of circumstances. At the period of the formation of the Nationalist group, consisting of Balakiref and his colleagues, in the earliest 'sixties, the Russian people as a whole had recently turned thinker, and as a result of the Emancipation of Serfs self-expression seemed the paramount duty of all. The awakening of socialistic thought resulted in the choice of a realistic and rationalistic mode of expression. In painting, perhaps the most startling manifestation was the work of Vereshchagin, whose pictures of war brought something like a realization of its awfulness to those who had never witnessed the horrors of the battlefield.

An artist less known to Britain, but of infinitely greater importance, is Repin, who ventilated, in some of his canvases, the grievances of Labour.

In literature, there was of course a similar movement, in which a leading place was taken by Chernishevsky's *What is to be Done?* but which is better described for the alien in the novels of Turgenef.

To discover the reflection of this current in music one need go no further than the realistic and humanistic documents left by Moussorgsky: *The Labourer's Lullaby, The Orphan, The Songs and Dances of Death* or *Boris Godounof,* the

National Music-Drama in which the hero is the people. The instrument or musical vehicle of expression in such times as these was naturally the voice, and opera, the most socialistic of art-forms, was a highly popular medium for the dissemination of liberal ideas.

With the advent of the 'eighties, continues Ossovsky, there came a reaction. The human form figured but rarely in pictures, and when seen at all was merely the peg on which to hang an abstract idea. With the education of the hitherto submerged came an appetite for idealistic art. In music the reign of realism came to an end, and even the " programme " began to be regarded as by no means an essential in the scheme of a symphonic work.

It is at this point in the history of Russian culture, of social evolution, and of musical development that Glazounof makes his appearance.

In this lies the explanation of his preference for the idealistic instrument, for using that instrument, even when employing it in the pictorial domain, in an idealistic rather than a realistic fashion, and, above all, for the development of its powers not as a band of individuals but as an indivisible whole.

(8)

In the æsthetic philosophy of Skryabin we meet frequently with the idea of materialization and dematerialization, of evolution and involution. According to the creator of *Prometheus* the arts find themselves alternately collected and fused, for the purpose of delivering a combined message, and dispersed for the individual development of each. In such a composer as Rimsky-Korsakof, particularly in the earlier works, we observe such a separation ; his players are encouraged, and the function of their instruments is gradually enlarged, by means of an increased responsibility. With Glazounof we arrive, on the contrary, at a dematerialization of the orchestra. Glazounof thinks in orchestral and not in instrumental terms. One might say that he appears to regard orchestration as an equivalent of self-consciousness. He would prefer to remain unconscious that, in writing for orchestra, he is engaged in a scientific pursuit. In his view, the ideal orchestral composer should be so completely at home with his materials that their successful distribution should give no more trouble than if he were writing for the single keyboard, and uniform *timbre*, of the piano. He has laid it down that a piece well orchestrated needs little or no rehearsal ; at the first trial it " goes well," at the second comes a fine performance. All this seems to be peculiarly fitting in a man for whom abstract beauty is the goal ; in Glazounof's symphonies, even when the programmatic element is present, that of the pictorial is kept in the background. The concrete is kept out of focus.

(9)

As a symphonic writer Glazounof has gradually drawn away from the use of external aids and has relied more and more on inherent beauty. Beginning with *Stenka Razin*—the work of a man who was reckoned, at the time of its composition, a powerful recruit to the nationalist coterie—he has progressed to the eighth symphony, which has earned him the title of " a contemporary classic master." As a half-way house in this process of evolution the fourth symphony (Opus 48), in E flat major, repays examination. In this we see the composer hesitating about his road. It contains reflections of the influence of Borodin in the Oriental theme (for English horn) of the Andante, of Liszt in its construction, its disregard of the four-movement form and the transformation of thematic substance, and of the West in the first subject (for oboe) of the Allegro moderato—a theme which is heard in several later works in a variety of guises, which do not, however, conceal its identity, notably in the concerto for violin.

At this stage the composer has already travelled

far ; on the road still before him he is to purify
the elements of his creative substance and to divest
it of everything which is not essentially musical.
" He has abandoned," says Rimsky-Korsakof in
his Memoirs, " the thickets of *The Forest* (Opus
19, dedicated to Stassof), the depths of *The Sea*
(Opus 28, dedicated to Wagner) and the walls of
The Kremlin " (Opus 30, dedicated to Moussorgsky) ; in the last-named the musical reflection of
the programme, indicated by headings, has become
quite faint ; the romanticism of the Andante of
the fifth symphony (Opus 55), of *Raymonda*
(Opus 57), of the sixth symphony (Opus 58), and
the *Middle Ages* suite (Opus 79) is not in the
vein of the contemporary descriptive composers ;
Glazounof has already gone far towards purging
himself, he is already nearing his promised land,
wherein music is absolutely self-sufficing, in the
seventh symphony. With the eighth he reaches
his destination.

This is not intended to imply that Glazounof
had forever renounced all musical forms outside
the region of the " absolute " or the purely symphonic. In his *Kalevala* suite (Opus 89), which
followed the *Finnish Fantasia*, he shows us that
he is not disposed to adopt the puristic attitude
of one who would divorce music from " programme." Of this we are, of course, assured by
his unwaning affection for the Ballet.

(10)

The development in Russia of the art of the Ballet has for the music-lover a very special interest because it has been instrumental in introducing to the notice of Western Europe the works of some remarkable musicians whose appearance among us might otherwise have been long delayed. In Russia the provision of music for the ballet has not been left to composers of the second rank, and to appreciate the full measure of Russian respect for the choreographic art, it is necessary only to attempt to picture for ourselves what would have been the bearing of a director of a Western European Conservatoire had he received an invitation to provide music for a ballet.

But in considering the entrance of music into this sphere of Drama we should exercise a little care in the formation of our judgments. It has been too frequently overlooked that there are many ballets of which the music was not written for the action put before us. At the recent production in Russia of the ballet *Stenka Razin*, in which Glazounof's music was used, it was complained that the symphonic movement did not coincide with the dramatic action. This is not, as might have been supposed, the fault of the composer, but of the producer, the music having been written many years before the ballet was designed.

Again, in the case of *Sheherazade*, a symphonic suite which is not intended, despite its printed synopsis, to describe in detail the narratives told her terrible liege by the sultana, we have, when witnessing the ballet, to bear in mind that the dramatic action has but the slenderest relation to the story which inspired the music ; the designer of the ballet has fitted one particular story to a piece of music that was associated in the composer's mind with the weaving of numberless tales. And so, if we discover a want of agreement between the stage occurrences and the symphonic commentary, it is often the producer and not the composer that is to blame. We do not find fault with Weber if the Rose-Spectre's gyrations are not faithfully reflected by the strains of the enchanting *Invitation à la Valse*.

With Glazounof's music, however, there is, for two reasons, a smaller risk of disagreement. Since *Stenka Razin* was written (in 1885) he has made some important contributions to the theatre ; *Raymonda*, *Ruses of Love* and *The Seasons* were directly designed as ballet music ; he has lately finished a further work, *The Love of Three Kings*. On the other hand we have in Glazounof a composer, as has been said, who does not choose to write in a deliberately descriptive style, and on this account one thinks of him as one whose art is particularly well-fitted for the purposes of the ballet. In the modern example the dancer seems less and less inclined to indulge in detailed descriptiveness, more and more towards making of the ballet a decorative thing, an inclination culminating in the postures of the Greek vase. In Glazounof, then, the modern ballet-artist should find a composer whose demands upon the histrion are few; the dance may remain as unfettered by duties towards the music as is Glazounof's music free from obligations to his stated programme. Finally, as a powerful instrument in the evocation of abstract emotions, Glazounof's facility in obtaining the finer gradations of orchestral colour is, in relation to his work as a composer of Russian ballet-music, a priceless gift.

(11)

Turning in despair from a contemplation of the British "graveyard" school of composition, an epithet bestowed, towards the close of the nineteenth century, upon the composers of interminable and dreary symphonic works, an English critic expressed his opinion that the British musical gift was more apparent in comic than in serious music. He averred that the British clown had never been equalled, that our music-hall comedians were in demand the world over, and that the British composer would never "find himself " until he realized that his true *métier* was the " vaudeville."

While one cannot unreservedly subscribe to a demand for such a drastic modification of ideals, one is able to perceive that a school of musicians may easily go astray and devote itself to a form of art for which it has in reality no vocation. For those who would welcome the appearance of the British School in some distinctive and completely national art-form, there remains always the difficulty of inventing such a form. One of our national traditions is a preference for things as they are, and it has perhaps been inevitable that our young musicians should for generations have reverenced the traditional symphonic form, the oratorio, and the classical quartet, as the types of music by means of which the self-respecting composer could best express himself. Of late, thanks to influences from abroad, it has seemed likely that the novice may be encouraged to try his hand at a kind of miniature opera, in which the spectacular is a negligible quantity, and in the ballet, where for the most part lightness of heart can prevail with perfect appropriateness.

In Russia such a problem presented itself in the earliest days of its musical history. It was Glinka who first awoke to the realization that, if the " broad public " was to be won over to dignified music, it could only be effected by means of some form of symphonic music less ponderous than the classical symphony. Hence the Caprice on Spanish themes, the *Jota Aragonesa*, and *Kamarinskaya*, the last-named work having many prototypes in Russian music.

The turn of chamber-music came with the establishment of the Belayef Circle of which the great patron of Russian music was, so to speak, a performing member. At the weekly evenings of the Circle it was customary to play over the various examples submitted for publication by the non-commercial firm over which Belayef presided. These gatherings appear to have been often highly convivial, and there were occasions, no doubt, on which no part of the proceedings could have been considered an appropriate moment for the introduction of severely formal chamber-music. As a consequence, works of another nature came into being, and it became gradually quite easy to reconcile the at first seemingly incongruous association of light music with a string quartet of earnest musicians.

Without having, in any sense, the character of a musical joke, such examples as the " Friday " series of small pieces for string quartet, the variations by a number of composers on a popular Russian theme, the " Belayef " (B. La. F.) and " Birthday " quartets are tokens of the spirit of *camaraderie* prevailing at these meetings, and thus inaugurate a new type of chamber-music to which, be it said, certain British examples of recent date conform. The innovation was instituted in a fashion somewhat less deliberate than that of the Fantasy form revived by Mr. Cobbett, but in other respects was equivalent.

(12)

In contemplating the chamber-music of Glazounof it is easily seen that though an orthodox composer, one, indeed, who is the principal representative of Russian musical academicism, there has been a ready disposition to fall in with this new attitude towards the old-established combination. We observe that the composer of eight symphonies is not ashamed to be represented in a collective work like the " Fridays " by pieces of a lighter order. The *Prelude* and *Fugue* with which the series opens remind us that this is the Glazounof of the symphonies, but they serve also to excite our wonder that he should be capable of his share in the Polka in D—the work of three different composers.

If these circumstances are taken into account the mood of Glazounof's chamber-music as a whole is more easily understood. One is less likely to wonder that the academicist, the " contemporary classicist," has not felt obliged to write quartets of a strictly classical pattern. Glazounof has been called a reactionary. In much of his chamber-music he looks back far beyond Brahms, and has written movements as jolly as those of Haydn of old.

But it is not as mere jolliness that one would characterize this part of Glazounof's product. One is less struck by the bustling passages of the *Scherzo*, in Opus 1, or the spirit of the *Slavonic Festival* (No. 4 of Opus 26), or the splendid vitality of the *Scherzo* of Opus 64, than by the beautiful specimens of spontaneous lyricism—a quality more often observed in the composer's chamber-music than in any other of the creative regions he has entered. The brief Andante of Opus 1, which is rather Mendelssohnian in character, gives only a foretaste of the banquet of melody the composer offers us in the five Novelettes, the Slav quartet, and the superb Adagio (con licenza) of the fifth example, a movement that gains something through its proximity to a particularly academic Allegro.

As in other spheres of composition, Glazounof exercises his native restraint when dealing with the string quartet. Although a master of the orchestra, he rarely displays the tendency, so frequently observable in Tchaikovsky, to allow his music to become orchestral in tonal bulk. Appropriateness is evidently an essential component of beauty. Only in the Slav quartet do we find him indulging in heavy chords calling upon the full capacity of the instruments, and forsaking the polyphonic method of writing which is so much more suitable to the slender tonal resources of the traditional quartet combination.

Glazounof's chamber-music has for many years held an honoured place. If it is not destined for immortality it may at least lay claim to have assisted in dispelling the quite prevalent illusion that modern chamber-music must of necessity be profound and obscure.

(13)

Glazounof began his career as a choral composer with the Triumphal March which was commissioned by the Committee of the Chicago Exhibition in 1895, and his subsequent essays in this form have partaken largely of the nature of *pièces d'occasion*. The initial effort has little interest beyond its testimony to a Wagnerian influence upon the Russian composer at this stage. The Coronation Cantata does not suggest that Glazounof was deeply inspired by the event he celebrates. The Memorial Cantata, performed at Leeds Festival in 1901, commemorates the birth of Pushkin, but the composer has chosen to perpetuate the memory of the great national poet in a fashion which suggests that the universality of the singer's fame, referred to by the Grand Duke Constantine (who provided the text), has attracted him more than the services rendered by Pushkin to his native country. Glazounof is also the composer of a work in memory of the celebrated sculptor, Antokolsky, but in this case the choral responsibility has fallen upon the shoulders of Lyadof, who furnished the second of the two movements.

We are able, however, to obtain from a more or less recent work a view of Glazounof, not as a writer of detached movements for chorus, but as the creator of incidental music, both choral and instrumental, for a drama of important dimensions. For the late Grand Duke Constantine's Passion Play, *The King of the Jews*, Glazounof wrote some music that, while adding a great deal to the somewhat slender merits of the royal playwright's effort, has brought a new distinction to the composer, and this music has been hailed with pleasure in Russia as the harbinger of the long-awaited opera from the pen of the central personage in the musical world. Owing to the official attitude of disapproval towards any representation of scriptural figures on the stage, the Grand Duke was obliged to leave several important episodes to the imagination of his audience. It is here that the descriptive power of music has been put to the test, and, despite his former aloofness from detail in music of the programmatic type, Glazounof scores a notable victory, and thereby achieves success for the whole drama. To mention one out of many places in which the music has made itself an indispensable factor, one may cite the unseen revelry that mocks the fallen Christ. In his music to this episode of the third act, Glazounof shows us not only that he has in a high degree the faculty of writing pictorial music, but that he is able to adapt the Lisztian method of thematic metamorphosis for employment in a new sphere. The followers of Pilate are made to mock by means of a figure which, in other parts of the drama, has a completely different significance. As might be supposed, *The King of the Jews* provides abundant opportunity for introducing music of an Oriental type, and by superb numbers, such as the Syrian dance, we are assured that the Eastern colouring observed in the composer's earlier works has not yet been exhausted—the colour is, if anything, warmer.

A fear to the contrary might well have been aroused by Glazounof's songs. In these, since his initial effort, there is neither lyrical nor harmonic warmth. They have certainly no particular melodic charm—that of Pushkin's drinking song, in mazurka rhythm, is a charm of a rather low order—and they do not possess the saving grace of harmonic wealth that brings to the vocal works of Rimsky-Korsakof a little greater distinction than would otherwise be theirs. Glazounof's examples are varied in style and range from tributes to Petrarch to a Venetian barcarolle, but they rarely rise above an ordinary level and are sometimes positively banal.

STRAVINSKY

CHAPTER IV

STRAVINSKY

(1)

WHILE in the death of Skryabin Russian music would seem to have suffered a grievous loss, the long interruption, caused by the war, of the growth of our acquaintance with the art of Stravinsky, is, from our point of view, no less serious. These two composers had hardly anything in common, so far as concerns the actual content of their music, but in their artistic outlook they shared the desire to seek for new means and modes of musical expression. Having discovered them, each met with that profound distrust of the unfamiliar which characterizes the attitude of the musical public as a whole, and both counted, no doubt, on securing the respectful hearing which is accorded the pioneer when the mass has learned that he is neither the fool nor the wag he was at first supposed to be.

In respect of the dead Skryabin we have to do with an artist who stood on the brink, if not of a great discovery, of an interesting experiment, one which can hardly have failed to widen the boundaries of the musical art had it been carried out.

I

Even if, through the dissemination of Skryabin's ideas, some living artist is impelled to make such an experiment on his own behalf, we should be justified in believing that his work must lack some measure of the profound inspiration needful for success.

But in Stravinsky's case the matter is perhaps even more serious. His is a young and vigorous mind whose eye peers into the future, and while he is in advance of contemporary musical opinion and judgment, we are assured, by the change of attitude towards one or two of his earlier works, that he has won a respectful attention and that he is now numbered among the greatest of contemporary masters.

There is, however, one aspect in particular of this composer which renders the absence of his music from our war-time musical life very regrettable, namely, that he, most of all the fine creative artists of Russia, represents in his art the Slavonic soul. No other Russian composer so faithfully carries on the tradition established by the Father of Russian music, and no other realizes so fully the meaning of the dictum of Moussorgsky that music must continue to reflect our human evolution, or die. Of late years there have been one or two totally ingenuous experiments destined to perpetuate the nationalist tradition. But the composers of operas consisting entirely of crude folk-song have overlooked the circumstance that such experiments belong to a past age, that musical Russia has experienced both the exploitation of pure folk-song and its secondary employment either as basic substance or as material only to be used for illustrative purposes ; in a word, that Russian musical society, having grown out of " Italianomania," has no further need of such primitive weapons of protest against this dead and buried enemy.

Stravinsky is guilty of no such misconception. He is a man of the Time, he has not failed to understand the function of music in its relation to humanity, and he appears to cherish a profound belief (and it is not surprising that he should) in the possibility of composing music that is significant both as music and as an expression of race.

These qualities render it highly important that we should keep ourselves in touch with the work of such an artist. Under present conditions, however, his progressive mind continues to evolve, whilst we, since the shock occasioned by the sights and sounds of his *The Rite of Spring*, have heard little that can help us to follow the path which he treads. We are thus in danger of finding, when once again we hear one of his recent works, that his music is still more remote from our understanding even than formerly, and as we are no longer in doubt as to either his sanity or his good faith one cannot help regarding the present lapse as something quite calamitous.

(2)

What are the characteristics that render Stravinsky one of the most important composers of the day ?

In nothing is the spirit of an age so clearly reflected as in its humour. In humour and its verbal expression we are able to trace that process of materialization and dematerialization which characterizes the progress of everything in the Universe. If we glance at the pages of British literature we have no difficulty in discerning the symptoms of this process. To recognize its workings we have only to compare the emphasis with which Dickens finds it necessary to underline a ridiculous situation or personal attribute, with the lightness of touch and pregnancy of phrase in the descriptive language of a Browning, a Meredith, or a Kipling, and then to observe the combination of the heavier with the lighter method to be discovered in the unstylish Chesterton. It should be obvious that over and above the meaning of Buffon's identification of the man with his style, there is to be taken into account the style of the man as an expression of the time in which he lived. Stravinsky's laconicism in music is not unlike the laconicism in present-day Cockney humour ; its enjoyment consists in bridging gaps.

It is not in the mere manipulation of the raw material of humour that Stravinsky excels, but in the method of making the very association of music and comedy a thing humoristic in itself. It is this faculty, united with a complete musicianship, that makes of *Petroushka* and *The Nightingale* an exceedingly significant contribution to the musico-dramatic literature of the age.

And what are the features of the nationalistic quality attributed to Stravinsky?

The answer to this question is to be found in the subjects of *The Fire-Bird* or *The Rite of Spring*, and in the score of *Petroushka*. In the first we have an example of the fantastic folk-lore subject of the kind first referred to by Glinka, and since by many another Russian composer. The Fire-bird was to have been the central figure in the opera which Balakiref sketched out, but did not develop, and the terrible Kashchei appears not only as the titular personage of Rimsky-Korsakof's opera but in his opera-ballet *Mlada*, and, by implication, in Moussorgsky's *Night on the Bare Mountain*. It is in *Mlada*, as in other of Rimsky-Korsakof's dramatic works, that we see the forerunner of *The Rite of Spring*, and it is by means of this work that Stravinsky once again calls attention to the connection between folk-song and pagan worship, an association to which his pantheist master so dearly loved to refer. Even in *The Nightingale*—a fairy-tale with a far-eastern subject related by a Scandinavian—there is felt the touch of one who shares the desire of Glinka to write for his countrymen in such a manner as to make them " feel at home." It is seemingly but a slight matter, and yet, if we put ourselves in the place of the Russian, long resident in England, who listens to the song of Death from the lips, not of the male to whom a Briton would have allotted the part, but from those of a feminine vocalist, we shall realize that this is one of the many details which together form the substance of a national dramatic art.

(3)

Near to the palace of Oranienbaum—built for Peter the Great by Menshikof, pastry-cook's apprentice become premier—lived Feodor Ignatievich Stravinsky, the successor of Petrof in the rôle of Pushkin's monk Varlaam (Boris Godounof), a singer of many bass parts at the Maryinsky Theatre. On January 29th, 1882, he took part, as King Frost, in Rimsky-Korsakof's splendid opera, *The Snow-Maiden*—a proud enough memory to mark that year. But a further and equally auspicious event was to occur, and, on June 5th, his son Igor was born. To what extent environment contributed to the development of the child's musical taste has not been directly revealed, but as it is recorded that his father was a good actor and artist, and as he does not appear to have been capable of the solecism attributed to one of his fellow-singers in *The Snow-Maiden*—of suggesting to its composer that one of its acts should conclude at a moment following a popular solo in order to secure applause—we may suppose that the parental attitude towards the musical art was such as to set a good example to the little Igor. It is clear, however, that the boy's father did not foresee a musical career for his child, for, despite the appearance of a distinct aptitude, the future composer of *Petroushka* was educated with a view of entrance into a legal calling. He was allowed, nevertheless, to cultivate his taste for music and his decided talent for the piano, which was fostered under the guidance of a pupil of Rubinstein.

Not until he was twenty does he appear to have begun to think seriously of carving out for himself a career in the musical world. Apparently the turning point was reached when, in 1902, whilst travelling abroad, he fell in with the composer of *The Snow-Maiden*, at Heidelberg, where Rimsky-Korsakof was spending the summer and devoting himself partly to his student son and partly to the composition of *Pan Voyevoda*. This meeting evidently made a great impression on young

Stravinsky, and it must have been the talks which he was privileged to have with the great teacher that led him to seek an all-round knowledge of the arts. One may safely assume that the same circumstance is responsible for the awakening of the latent creative gift, for in the following year Stravinsky engaged on the composition of a piano sonata in four movements, the latter three of which were completed a little later. It was with this earnest of his powers that he now approached Rimsky-Korsakof and secured the latter's consent to undertake their cultivation. In Korsakof's *Memoirs of My Musical Life* there is no mention of Stravinsky, but it is asserted by M. Vuillermoz that the teacher was unable to conceal a certain satisfaction aroused by Stravinsky's revolutionary ideas, and the French critic further states that the contrast between the views of this somewhat restive pupil and those of the more docile students then under his care was not an unpleasant one. It is difficult to deny oneself the conjecture as to whether, in expressing the quite unorthodox opinion on the subject of Bach's *Johannes Passion*, recorded in 1904 in his diary, Rimsky-Korsakof was inspired, in his revolt against the prevailing acceptation of all the classic masterpieces at their original valuation, by the bold heterodoxy of his disciple. Whatever may have been the effect of Korsakof's contact with this fresh young mind we are at least able to trace, with some certainty, the influence of the master, especially in the region of orchestration, a subject studied by the novice under the same guidance during 1905 and the following year. It is said that one of the exercises prescribed was the re-scoring of the piano arrangement of *Pan Voyevoda*, the result being subsequently compared with the composer's own version.

(4)

Until the time of his marriage (in January, 1906) it seems that Stravinsky, although close on twenty-four years of age, had not definitely resolved to devote himself wholly to composition. On this step he now decided. A symphony, completed a year after his entry into the matrimonial estate, and performed by the Court orchestra (but withheld from publication until some years later), was the first fruit of the so-to-say consecrated activities.

By 1908 he had already made a considerable addition to his output. The suite for voice and orchestra, on Pushkin's imitation of de Parny—the bucolic poem, *Faun and Shepherdess*—written by the schoolboy poet when still an ardent admirer of the "French Tibullus"; the orchestral *Fantastic Scherzo*, inspired by Maeterlinck's *Life*

of the Bee, the two songs to texts from the verse
of Sergei Gorodetsky, one of Gorky's early asso-
ciates, and the four piano studies testify to the
catholicity of the composer's tastes, both literary
and musical, at this time. The dedication of two
of the piano pieces to the sons of Rimsky-Korsakof
suggest a happy relationship with his teacher's
family, but this was now severed by death. The
composition of the since popularized *Fireworks*
was inspired by Stravinsky's wish to contribute to
the festivities on the occasion of the marriage of
Rimsky-Korsakof's daughter Sonia to M. Steinberg, the composer of *Midas*. The manuscript
was delivered, but the eyes for which it was intended were closed for ever. The young composer's next work was also of a commemorative
kind, but of quite a different nature. The *Funeral
Song*, written in honour of his deceased friend and
master, was subsequently performed at one of
Belayef's Russian Symphony Concerts.

Hardly had this memorable chapter in Stravinsky's life been closed than the first page of
another, in which he was to exchange the rôle of
pupil for that of teacher, was being written.
During the summer of the year following that of
Rimsky-Korsakof's death he was engaged upon the
first part of the famous *Nightingale*. It was whilst
occupied with this that the attention of Diaghilef
was drawn to his young compatriot's gift. In the

composition of the music of a ballet founded on the old Russian legendary subject of *The Fire-Bird*, which Diaghilef commissioned him to write, Stravinsky had a task which he had doubtless been taught by Rimsky-Korsakof to love. The score, the first token of the young musician's fitness to wear the mantle of Glinka, was ready in May, 1910, and on June 25th of that year Paris paid, at the Grand Opera, the first of several tributes to the young Russian.

It is to Diaghilef that we are indebted for our knowledge of Stravinsky's art, and to another Russian for our earliest introduction to Moussourgsky. But France must have the credit in both cases of having sponsored the works of these two prophets, both of whom failed to secure a due honour at home. Little wonder that Stravinsky should have found inspiration in the neighbourhood of La Baule to join the ranks of the many distinguished French musicians who have celebrated Verlaine. Belonging to the period that saw the composition of the two songs on texts by the unhappy author of the *Fêtes Galantes*, is the performance in Paris of *Fireworks*, the symphonic *pièce d'occasion* already referred to, an event which marks the date of the composer's full recognition, both by the public and by his colleagues in France.

(5)

Having thoroughly established himself in the hearts of the Parisians, Stravinsky began a period of wanderings, visiting in turn Switzerland, the Riviera and Italy. But if he acquired the outward qualities of the cosmopolitan, his musical soul had not lost contact with his native land. During these travels he framed the action and wrote the music of his masterpiece. *Petroushka* was finished in Rome in May, 1911, and, just about a year after the first performance of *The Fire-Bird* was produced at the Chatelet Theatre, Paris, with tremendous success. Both ballets have since made the tour of Europe, and have received tardy recognition in the two Russian capitals.

If the influence of environment were really of great importance to the conception of such a work, *Petroushka* should certainly have been conceived in Petrograd ; but it was at Clarens that this work first took shape.

Stravinsky, following the precedent set up by Tchaikovsky and observed by Skryabin, who had not long left the neighbourhood of Lausanne, established himself in Switzerland after the above-recorded Odyssey, and made his home at Clarens for a considerable time. All three composers appear to have been inspired during their stay in this country to give a mystical quality to their art.

Here Tchaikovsky sought a frame of mind meet for the composition of his *Joan of Arc*; on the same shore of Lake Geneva the composer of *Prometheus* gave much thought to the subject of his projected, but never completed, " Mystery," and at Clarens it was that Stravinsky revealed the first symptoms of a dramatic mysticism which has since led some to believe that the composer received suggestions from Rimsky-Korsakof other than those in respect of purely technical matters. His first labour in the new home was apparently upon the sacred Cantata *Zviezdoliky*, which may well have been inspired by *Mlada*, and is to be regarded as a fore-runner of the *Rite of Spring*. In the two settings of Balmont, also an exile, but an involuntary one, there is again a mystical quality. These songs were written, however, not at Clarens, but during a stay at the composer's estate at Oustiloug in Volhynia, which has since been the scene of much devastation. The first of the three curious Japan-ese lyrics for voice and orchestra was begun here in 1912, the series being completed on the return to Clarens in the following year.

In *The Rite of Spring*, for the first performance of which Stravinsky once more sought Paris, is to be discovered the culmination of the tendency, first manifested in *Zviezdoliky*, and despite the experiences through which France has since passed its production can hardly have been forgotten.

From mysticism of a spiritual kind Stravinsky turned to a sort of sociological symbolism, reviving for his theme a subject, that of Andersen's tale, *The Nightingale*, abandoned some years previously after the writing of one part. This, as will be remembered, was produced somewhat inadequately at Sir Joseph Beecham's memorable Russian season at Drury Lane in 1914, when the composer was present.

Since that time Stravinsky has shown no disposition to rest on his laurels. Already there are three works which are unknown to us, one of them spiritual, another, *Svadebka*, having associations, like *The Rite of Spring*, with ancient Russian festive practices, and a suite of three pieces for string quartet which has been produced in America.

It seems possible, if not altogether likely, that as a result of a stimulus to the expression of national feeling created by the war, Russian composers may desire to revive the more direct methods of nationalizing their music. But even in that event the methods of the early 'sixties can hardly be expected to appeal to the new world, and it seems certain that the twentieth-century Russian nationalists will introduce the desired element in a manner a little less obvious than those of the nineteenth. At the present time there is no Russian composer who knows better what is needed than Igor Stravinsky.

(6)

In their presentation of ballets before the Western European musical and dramatic world, the Russians have risked a failure to enlist our serious attention. The countrymen of Dargomijsky and Moussorgsky might have been expected to eschew the lapses from legitimacy and verity which it was the aim of these two composers to condemn and repair in such works as *The Stone Guest* and *Boris Godounof*. It might also have been supposed that a Russian whose mission is apparently that of proving the superiority of the national art-product, would be the first to recognize the reformative movement with which such institutions as the Moscow Art-Theatre have been associated, and the last to countenance such a wilful disregard of the musico-dramatic proprieties as has been manifested in several of the ballet productions presented in Paris and London. In these we have seen music degraded for the purposes of the dance in a manner which could hardly have commended itself to the founders of the Modern Russian School, and should not have been adopted by anyone desirous of being considered worthy to have control of the destinies of such an art as the modern ballet. Not content with announcing the music of the ballets *Sheherazade, Antar* and *Tamara*, as if it had actually been written by its composers for that specific purpose, these organizers have, in the case of the first-named, taken music composed to a specified programme and have adapted it for an entirely different " plot," without so much as an explanation. Taking a slender trifle of Chopin, moreover, they have mated it to a choreographic monster that requires several repetitions of the delicate little piece, and thus, by giving to a handmaiden the work of a slut, have contrived to wear away its original exquisite charm.

In the sphere of art-dancing we have learned a great deal from its Russian exponents, but their treatment of music as an allied art rather painfully recalls the older form of ballet from which one would have thought that the Slavs would try to dissociate themselves.

(7)

When we come, however, to the consideration of the ballets of which the music has been contributed by Stravinsky, we are confronted with works of a very different kind. We know that in the construction of these ballets the composer has taken a very prominent and active part, that when he has not actually been responsible for the arrangement of the *scenario*, as appears to have been the case in *The Rite of Spring*, his views have

STRAVINSKY.

been welcomed and adopted, and that all the music has been written for the single purpose of heightening the significance of the stage-play, and for no other. One imagines, too, that Stravinsky has done his utmost to secure for music a position of dignity in the general scheme of the ballet, for, in comparing his three works in this form, we observe that whereas in *The Fire-Bird* the orchestra supplies the usual musical commentary upon the dramatic action, though on occasion taking upon itself a function which renders it something more than an accessory, in the second work, *Petroushka*, the dramatic action depends so largely upon episodes in which the dance is no longer accessory but essential, that music becomes a vital necessity to the scheme. Finally, in *The Rite of Spring* there is an entire absence of anything in the nature of drama ; what we are called upon to contemplate is not a ballet-drama in which the action is rendered in terms of the dance, but a reproduction of pre-historic worship in which the dance, and not the play, is "the thing," and which to our twentieth-century perceptions would be almost meaningless were it divorced from the ample rhythmic suggestions provided for us by Stravinsky.

We have thus in Stravinsky not a mere composer of music for this or that ballet, whose pen is at the service of anyone having a commission to offer, but a reformative force whose labours are directed towards the emancipation, or at least the salvation, of music from a danger by which it seems to be constantly menaced. If, therefore, we wish to regard the ballet as a province in which music may legitimately be employed, we are bound to accord to Stravinsky a place in the Valhalla of heroes now occupied by such as Monteverde, Gluck, Wagner, Dargomijsky, Moussorgsky and Debussy.

But this is not the only kind of tribute due to him. It has already been hinted that Stravinsky is regarded, in the opinion of many, as the last hope of Russian musical nationalism. It would not be in excess of the facts to maintain that in his choreographic works Stravinsky has provided for our consideration a modern type of nationalistic music which has every right to be placed on a level with Glinka's *A Life for the Tsar*, Moussorgsky's *Boris Godounof*, or Rimsky-Korsakof's *The Snow-Maiden*. Neither of his three ballets resembles either of the works quoted in any particular beyond a general nationalistic import ; but it is not difficult to point to individual works of the New Russian School, of which two of Stravinsky's choreodramas are to be considered as prototypes. The story of *The Fire-Bird* is substantially that of Rimsky-Korsakof's *Kashchei the Immortal*, while that of *The Rite of Spring*, as has already been suggested, must surely have been inspired by the same composer's *Mlada*, and perhaps by certain passages in *The Snow-Maiden*. As to *Petroushka*, if its dramatic action has no prototype in Russian music-drama, its music owes much to the precept of Stravinsky's forerunners, beginning with Glinka.

(8)

In identifying the literary basis of *The Fire-Bird* with that of Korsakof's *Kashchei*, it should be pointed out that the latter work is but a *pastiche* of episodes derived from legendary lore, with the monster as a central figure. In Stravinsky's ballet the ogre is an accessory character, so far as concerns the dramatic action, but his presence in the scheme is nevertheless vital to it.

Ivan Tsarevich, the hero of many tales, wandering in the night, espies the Fire-Bird attempting to pluck the golden fruit from a silver tree, and, after a chase, succeeds in capturing her. But receiving the gift of a glowing feather he consents to forgo his prize. As the darkness of night lifts, Ivan discovers that he is in the grounds of an old castle, from which thirteen maidens presently emerge. They are observed by the concealed youth to make play with the tree and its fruit. Disclosing himself, he obtains possession of a golden apple. With the approaching dawn the maidens withdraw into the castle, which Ivan now recognizes as that of the fearsome Kashchei, captor of decoyed travellers, over whom he tyrannously wields his magic power. Ivan resolves upon entering Kashchei's abode, but on opening the gate he is confronted first by a motley horde of freakish monsters and then by the ogre himself, to whose court they belong. Kashchei seeks to bewitch the young adventurer and to turn him to stone, but Ivan is protected by the glowing feather. Presently the bird comes to his aid and nullifies Kashchei's threatened spell, and, after demonstrating its power by causing the frightful company of courtiers to break into a frenzied dance, reveals the casket in which Kashchei's " death " is hidden. From the casket Ivan takes an egg, which he dashes to the ground ; the death it contains unites itself with its owner and the dread wizard dies. His castle vanishes, his victims are liberated, and Ivan receives the hand of the most beautiful of the maidens.

The music of the ballet describes with an extraordinary wealth of suggestion the various weird figures of the drama, and is of a nature never allowing us to forget that it is fantasy and not life that we are witnessing. The flight of the Fire-Bird, its dance, and its vain resistance are rendered in music whose primary purpose is the description of movement and not descriptiveness itself, while the quarry's pleading is brought to our ears through a veil of make-believe; her supplication is in accents that suggest the conventional posturing of the *ballerina* and not of a real bird ensnared. Throughout the ballet the music serves as a preparation, by means of the ear, for what the eye is to witness. Even the graceful nocturnal dance of the captive maidens has a note that suggests the dominion of their villainous gaoler, and the episodic theme of their play with the apples is that which later heralds their liberation through the good graces of the Fire-Bird. Ere the delightful melody of the *Khorovode* has died away we are aware that we shall soon have something less dainty to contemplate, and, with the approach of the monster and his awful satellites, it is clear that another musical picture is to be added to the gallery inaugurated by Glinka with his March of Chernomor in *Russlan and Ludmilla*.

The Fire-Bird, having been completed in 1910, contains little music that can be compared with the pages of the bolder Stravinsky to be seen in *The Nightingale*, and it provides moments of genuine melodic charm, a quality upon which the composer has ceased to rely. Of such is the maidens' *Khorovode*. In the Tsarevna's lullaby, rocking her into a sleep that will protect her from the doomed Kashchei, Stravinsky already hints at his independence. But with him, the process of advancement does not appear to involve a departure from the nationalistic tradition, and the page in which, with music of a folk-nature and a modal kind, he describes the appearance of Ivan before the maidens, he seems to foretell that the development of his whole strength will not be allowed to disturb the roots of his art.

(9)

The " plot " of *Petroushka* owes nothing to folk-lore, but retains the quality of the fantastic. Its chief protagonist is a lovelorn doll; but we have still a villain in the person of the *focusnik*, a showman who, for his own ends, prefers to consider that a puppet has no soul. The scene is the Admiralty Square, Petrograd; the time, " Butter-week," somewhere about the eighteen-thirties. Two curtains are used in the performance of this ballet; the first is a barrier between the real public and the presenters of the ballet; the second is that which divides the showman's drama from both the stage crowd and the people in the outer theatre. Prior to the raising of the first, the music has an expectant character, and the varied rhythmic treatment of a melodic figure which has a distinct folk-tune flavour has all the air of inviting conjecture as to what is about to happen.

Once the curtain goes up we are immediately aware that we are in the midst of a carnival, and are prepared for some strange sights. The music describes the nature of the crowd magnificently, and in his orchestral reproduction of a hurdy-gurdy, whose player mingles with the throng, Stravinsky has taken pains that his orchestral medium shall not lend any undue dignity to the instrument. When a rival musical-box appears on the other side of the stage Stravinsky shows us, by the combination of the diverse musical elements coming from the two organs and the orchestral reflection of the stage movement, what the Russian composer has learned from the example provided by Glinka's *Kamarinskaya*. Presently the showman begins to attract his audience, and, preparatory to opening his curtain, plays a few mildly florid passages on his flute. With his final flourish he animates his puppets. They have been endowed by the showman with human feelings and passions. Petroushka is ugly and consequently the most sensitive. He endeavours to console himself for his master's cruelty by exciting the sympathy and winning the love of his fellow-doll, the Ballerina, but in this he is less successful than the callous and brutal Moor, the remaining unit in the trio of puppets. Jealousy between Petroushka and the Moor is the cause of the tragedy which ends in the pursuit and slaughter of the former. The Russian Dance, which the three puppets perform at the bidding of their taskmaster, recalls so vividly the passage of a crowd in Rimsky-Korsakof's *Kitej* that one can hardly permit oneself the use of so mild a term as "influence." It is, in respect both of rhythm and melodic structure, a reproduction. But Stravinsky's individual harmonic treatment clothes it most appropriately for its present purpose.

When, at the end of the Dance, the light fails and the inner curtain falls, we are reminded by the roll of the side-drum which does duty as *entr'acte* music that we have to do with a realist, with a composer who is no more inclined than was his precursor Dargomijsky to make concessions ; he prefers to preserve illusions and so long as the drum continues its slow fusillade the audience's mind is kept fixed upon the doll it has been contemplating. The unsuccessful courtship is now enacted and then the scene is again changed to the Moor's apartment, where, after a monotonous droning dance, the captivation of the Ballerina takes place. There are, from time to time, musical figures recalling the showman's flute flourishes, apparently referring to his dominion over the dolls. The deliciously crude sentimentality of the slow Valse danced by the black and white pair is as characteristic a product of Stravinsky's humour as is the fragmentary allusion to Petroushka, whose appearance follows.

The scene ends with the summary ejection of that unfortunate, and the drum once more bridges the change of scene.

In the last tableau the Carnival, with its consecutive common-chords, is resumed. The nurses' dance, which is of folk origin, is one of several items of decorative music, some of them, like the episode of the man with the bear, and the merchant's accordion, being fragmentary. With the combined dance of the nurses, coachmen and grooms, we have again a wonderful counterpoint of the melodic elements.

When the fun is at its height it is suddenly interrupted by Petroushka's frenzied flight from the little theatre. He is pursued by the Moor, whom the cause of their jealousy tries vainly to hold in check. To the consternation of the spectators Petroushka is slain by a stroke of the cruel Moor's sword, and a tap on the *tambour de basque*.

The showman, having demonstrated to the satisfaction of the gay crowd that Petroushka is only a doll, is left alone with the corpse, but is not allowed to depart in absolute peace of mind. To the accompaniment of a ghastly distortion of the showman's flute music the wraith of Petroushka appears above the little booth. There is a brief reference to the carnival figure, then four concluding *pizzicato* notes and the drama is finished. From his part in outlining it we conclude that Stravinsky is an artist whose lightness of touch equals that of Ravel, whose humanity is as deep as Moussorgsky's.

(10)

The third of Stravinsky's ballets is a work of an entirely different order. As has been pointed out, the Dance is here exalted until it is the all-pervading element.

The ceremonial of *The Rite of Spring* is arranged in a fashion that allows of the music being worked up gradually to a final ecstatic climax, something similar to the culminating points discoverable in the later mystical sonatas of Skryabin. After some seventy bars of introduction the curtain rises on Roerich's extraordinary conception, a landscape that might well be designed to symbolize laconicism in scene-painting. In its foreground takes place the first part of the ceremonial, the worship of Earth. In this participate youths and maidens in robes of contrasted hues, and as part of the ritual there is a mock abduction followed by the spring *Khorovode* or *Rondo*. The music, which has been of a persuasive or sensuous kind, now subsides into a soberer mood, and there appears in procession the Sage, bearded to his ankles, his hair falling to his elbows. He prostrates himself before Nature, blessing the earth and imploring its fertility. The orchestral commentary is composed of a regularly sustained arrangement of three simultaneous rhythmic figures, which undergo little variation other than the dynamic.

In the second tableau the Sacrifice takes place. It opens with a mystical circular ceremonial, the maidens' movements being accompanied by a slow chant alternating with a measure having a dance character. Presently, while the sacrificial maiden is being elected, the dancing is arrested, but the music surges on into an ecstasy. For the glorification of the victim-elect there is a positive apotheosis of rhythm, the measure changing almost at every bar. The Evocation of Ancestors brings music which apparently represents the calling and listening of the supplicants. The sages demand the final ritual, the sacrificial dance begins, the maiden's movements simulate the joy of fertility, as though challenging Nature, and after reaching the culminating ecstasy, she collapses and expires. The Rite is consummated by her death.

The music of *The Rite of Spring* suggests the primitive, but it is not primitive music; it is the rendering of the primitive in terms of music. To have attempted to reproduce the actual

prehistorical would have been, literally, a prepos-
terous proceeding, since the purpose of the music
is that of reflecting, upon a twentieth-century
audience's temperament, the emotions of these
primeval pagan worshippers. In the melodic and
rhythmic fragments that suggest the sources of
the Russian folk-song Stravinsky has succeeded,
without committing any kind of anachronistic
solecism, in conveying to a modern audience an
impression of archaic element-worship among the
ancient Slavs, suggesting that there is a strong
link, not only between primitive and contemporary festive practices, but between primitive
and contemporary Russian music, a connection
which this composer strives hard to preserve.
Thus the advent of the maidens is accompanied
by a theme that is typically Russian, both as to
melody and rhythm, and the contour of the
Tranquillo which introduces the spring *Khorovode*
is similarly characteristic. Even the solid chord
blocks in the music of the initial Heralding of
Spring recalls the manner, though not the melody,
of the Russian Dance in *Petroushka*.

The circumstance that *The Rite of Spring* was
received on its production with scant favour has
little to do with its value. Our purpose at the
moment of its presentation was mainly that of
seeking entertainment. We were not then impelled by a sense of duty to seek an understanding

of the Slav character and of Russian racial history. We were impatient of explanation, and, deriving no immediate enjoyment from the music, dismissed the stage action as of no moment.

In *The Rite of Spring* Stravinsky gives us far more than we were then able or willing to appreciate. It is, in fact, the dramatic equivalent of Skryabin's " Mystery." That the congregational atmosphere was absent is no fault of the composer's.

(11)

From a composer who frankly expresses an aversion from the conventional operatic structural pattern, who believes that music " can be married to gesture or to words—but not to both, without bigamy," we do not expect opera in a stereotyped form. *The Nightingale* is not called an opera, but a Lyrical Tale in three acts ; its music is married neither to gesture nor to words, but to ideas, which the words do indeed convey, though quite indirectly. The music is wedded to satire ; it bears little relation to the words, and concerns itself almost exclusively with their intended meaning, neglecting their literal sense. Stravinsky, in setting Andersen's fairy-tale, might well have been thinking that the story was by Krilof, for his music really plays the part of the little explanatory paragraph with which the great Russian fabulist usually pointed a moral to his tale. The composer's procedure is not, of course, quite the same ; he does not reserve his music until the end, to be contained in one terse and ironical harmony, but through it he assures us that his art is not merely for art's sake, that it has a didactic purpose. His music provides the tone of voice in which the words are uttered, and the tone is satirical. One might say that while the tale is Andersen's, the manner of telling it is Krilof's. Russian satirists are partial to the nightingale as a symbol of true art ; whether, in causing the chief character in the drama to be invisible, Stravinsky was aiming a shaft at *prima-donnism* must be left to conjecture ! The plan followed by Mitoussof, the librettist, is drawn up with a fairly strict regard for the original story-teller's version, but the music tells the story with more point.

The Chinese Emperor is informed that the nightingale is a famous singer, and that its repute is justly earned. He and his court have often heard its note, but they have not hitherto been aware of the merit they are now assured it possesses. The only appreciative person in the whole Imperial company has been the little kitchen-maid through whom the nocturnal songster's gift is made known. There has also been a fisherman . . .

In the second act the nightingale, bidden to

court, gives a "command performance," and is made aware, by an offer of gold, that the Emperor has deigned to recognize her gift. Hardly has the fashion of singing been established among the courtiers, than news is brought that the Ruler of Japan has a still more remarkable nightingale, which he begs the Chinese Emperor to accept. The new singer has a covering of diamonds, and has to be wound up before it can perform. During its vocal flights, which appear to make a genuine impression upon the Emperor and his *entourage*, the real nightingale disappears in search of a more congenial environment. The monarch, wishing to make a comparison, is furious at this want of respect, and decrees that the offender shall be exiled. The fisherman knows that life without art is death. . . .

In the third act the Emperor is seen lying on his bed in mortal sickness, and near him sits the grim spectre Death. The monarch is troubled in spirit and invokes, like Saul, the balm of music. The voice of the nightingale is heard in compassionate response to his appeal. The song is of Death's garden, and Death is so moved by the nightingale's poetic description that the Emperor is relinquished to Life, and he expresses a wish that the songster shall remain forever at his beck and call. He is told that its music will always be near him. As for the courtiers, they have already accepted the

Emperor's demise as inevitable, and are much astonished when, during the funeral march to the weird strains of which they assemble in their sovereign's death-chamber, he puts his head through the bed-curtains and cheerfully greets them " Good morning." The fisherman's voice is heard greeting the dawn of a new life.

(12)

The music to *The Nightingale* was begun in 1909, the year of the production of *The Fire-Bird*. Its composition was interrupted for three years or so, and only finished early in 1914, when its composer's artistic outlook had undergone a complete change, as is shown by the intervening *Rite of Spring*—called by a Russian commentator a musical Chinese Wall which casts its shadow over the latter part of *The Nightingale*. But these circumstances are not so destructive of the homogeneity of that work as one might perhaps expect. In the first act, which constitutes the earlier portion, the dramatic situation is not on the whole in need of that more complex treatment required later on, when the rivalry between the real and the artificial singers is being portrayed. There is a need of contrast between the simplicity and artlessness of the earlier scene and the effect to be created by the Chinese March in Act II, and this Stravinsky is able to emphasize, thanks to his amazingly increased dexterity and inventiveness in the use of the orchestral instrument. The pentatonic figure, in three keys simultaneously, with which the composer begins the assembly of the Imperial court, lacks nothing of the *bizarre*, even to the ear of the most progressive musician, and serves to underline the change of scene which has taken place since the nightingale sang unselfconsciously to the humble fisherman. The song, too, is changed, and one fears that the singer is already losing something of that naturalness which so rarely survives such an experience.

The pathos of the last act, when the Emperor's crown and sceptre have already been appropriated by Death, admirably balances the dignity of that part of the first act in which the fisherman and the nightingale are in possession of the scene ; in the first passages given to the Bonze, when announcing to the nightingale that the Emperor has graciously consented to listen to a song during his next meal, the music begins its function of inserting, as it were, the satirical sense between the lines of the text, and in a somewhat different manner it certainly prepares us for the exquisite mock solemnity of the funeral march trodden by the unsuspecting and dutifully mourning courtiers. The final soliloquy of the fisherman, who is endowed by nature with a sense that makes him hear in the singing of the birds " the heavenly voice," is treated by Stravinsky in a fashion making it plain that if at first the operatic form was uncongenial to him there can be no doubt about his sympathy with this literary material.

(13)

It speaks volumes against the customary method of approaching a modernist composer's work that the names of Debussy and Stravinsky should in turn have been bracketed with that of Strauss. The Frenchman and the Russian have more than one common feature, both in the matter and the manner of their compositions, and especially that of the aim of simplifying and purifying the art-forms in which they choose to express themselves ; but the Teuton has in his more recent examples displayed a tendency to progress only in quantity, and has evinced a conspicuous lack of inventiveness. In other words, Strauss has chosen to hurl a tremendous orchestra at popular favour in order to conquer it by a sort of musical " frightfulness." It is true, that when swelling the number of instrumentalists in a group (and thereby decreasing the responsibility of the unit), he has added new types ; but even when these additions belong properly to the domain of music, as sometimes they do not, they have not been included for the purposes of an increased subtlety of expression, but merely to obtain a greater volume of sound.

Stravinsky

With Stravinsky, who, like Debussy, inherits the tendency to simplify from Dargomijsky (through Moussorgsky), there is on the contrary a constant striving for conciseness of musical statement, and for an increase of the responsibility of the orchestral unit. It is possible that the procedure followed in some places by Rimsky-Korsakof, of allotting solos even to the usually inconspicuous instruments, has influenced Stravinsky to seek a means of making the orchestra a more subtle and less cumbersome instrument. At any rate the aim is clearly to be recognized in the scoring of the works, whether big or small, which have been composed since the first symphony. An increase in bulk is accompanied by a significant increase in kind. If the community of his orchestra is extended, the number of families and groups becomes greater ; if the orchestra is a small one, the units are given work which makes their relation, one to the other, similar to that of the members of a string quartet. It is said, and, if it be true, it is well worthy of mention here, that in a recent work for the chamber-combination, he has aimed at an identification of an individual tone-colour with each instrument, which would appear to signify that not only would the 'cello be treated with a regard for its *tessitura* that would tend to keep it distinct from the viola at moments when they might be confused by the hearer, but also that the second violin would be written for as an instrument having a tone-character of its own, or at all events an individual melodic disposition.

In a composer of Stravinsky's mentality this search for precision seems highly appropriate. It is of course exceedingly gratifying that it should have fallen to a really progressive artist to show by what means simplification could be secured, other than the reaction to mere primitiveness which has so often been mooted as the only remedy for that *augmentum ad absurdum* threatened by advocates of the big orchestral battalions.

In the *Scherzo Fantastique* (Opus 3), we already perceive the refining process at work, and the composer is aided in the attainment of this end by the circumstance that the piece owes its inspiration to his enjoyment of Maeterlinck's *Life of the Bee*, a literary substance that immediately suggests a treatment on fine lines rather than in broad effects.

In the construction of the *Fire-Bird* orchestra there is further evidence of an intention to create every variety of effect suitable to this fantastic subject, and it is quite clear that piquancy, and not mere abundance of tone, is regarded by the composer as the desirable means, even when dealing with the monstrous figure of the terrible Kashchei.

And after a hearing of *The Nightingale* with its conspicuous economy in instrumentation—the more pleasing since it was produced at a time when the proper solution of the problem of ever-increasing bigness had not been grasped—it is with less surprise that we learn of a recent essay, *Svadebka*, in which, according to intelligence from abroad, Stravinsky has reduced the orchestra in the sense of enfranchising every instrumentalist, and has included in an orchestral body having a quite unusual number of parts, vocal instruments that have a tonal but not a verbal significance.

Stravinsky's orchestral work as a whole is a symptom of that constantly alternating aggregation and segregation of the arts, among themselves, and within each of them separately, of which we have already spoken. His views suggest that he is in favour of a temporary specialization, and his activities as an orchestral composer proclaim him to be the advocate of a better and more efficient instrument, both in its relation to music and in its handling by the individual. What form the reverse process, that must come after the desired refinements have been achieved, will take, it is difficult to guess.

(14)

The popular song episode in his rather academic first symphony is but a faint indication of that

subtle connection with the Fatherland with which
Stravinsky has contrived to endow almost all his
music. In his first published vocal piece—composed soon after his marriage and dedicated to his
wife—his national colour is of no deeper hue than
that constituted by the choice of part of Pushkin's
Faun and Shepherdess as the text of his suite for
voice and orchestra. In its three numbers, *The
Shepherdess*, *The Faun*, and *The Stream*, he con-
tents himself with music of a pastoral kind that
has nothing of a Slavonic flavour. But a year
later, when inspired by the verses of that ardent
young patriot, Serge Gorodetsky, to set this poet's
Spring, he wrote music in which the Russian bells
chime, hardly ceasing, throughout the song, and
even in *The Song of the Dew* (the second number
of this Opus 2), which includes a reference to the
Flagellants' mystic hymn, there is nothing quite
so suggestive.

Stravinsky is not the first musician to celebrate
his entrance into matrimony by writing for the
voice. When observing that the two Verlaine
numbers are dedicated to his brother, Goury
Stravinsky—a singer possessing the good taste as
well as the bass voice of his father—one assumes
that the composer did not regret that he had not
reserved his first dedication for his setting of
Verlaine's *La Lune Blanche*, an excerpt from the
ill-omened *Bonne Chanson*, the second of the two

texts furnished with music at La Baule in 1910. In selecting this classic, the Russian took a step which speaks volumes for his courage, since the greatest modern Frenchmen, in providing music to these words have given of their best, knowing that only their best was meet. But both in this and in the other little poem, *Un Grand Sommeil Noir*, from *Sagesse*, Stravinsky has not only proved himself worthy of the self-bestowed honour, but has written his music in a style that could easily pass as belonging to one of the poet's compatriots of a later generation. Their treatment prepares us for the manner of his subsequent vocal works, and, indeed, those written since the Verlaine examples are not to be successfully approached without preparation. His settings of Balmont's *Forget-Me-Not* and *The Pigeon* recall Moussorgsky's delicate suggestiveness and disregard of conventional form. In the latter is a particularly clear example of the method of writing harmonic passages in different streams or planes— a method associated with several modern composers besides Stravinsky.

In his most recent published songs, the *Three Japanese Lyrics*, with an accompaniment for a miniature orchestra, Stravinsky pays a tribute to France different in kind from that suggested in reference to the Verlaine numbers. They are dedicated to three distinguished French composers, Messrs. Maurice Delage, Florent Schmitt and Maurice Ravel. Apparently, the first-named — an expert orientalist — inspired these delicate little descriptive pages for which he supplied the texts. They are particularly interesting in that they are in remarkable contrast to the Oriental essays of the earlier Russians, who adopted a more or less conventional idiom in which the interval of the augmented second plays a conspicuous part. Stravinsky, going further east, breaks with the established convention, and does not rely for an instant upon the approved ingredients of Oriental colouring.

Almost throughout his creative work we observe this determination to dispense with everything stereotyped, whether reasonable or absurd. The musician who realizes that music is not intended to evoke echoes of past emotions, but to heighten present ones, should be assured of a prominent place when the new order of things has been installed. That is why one is confident that Stravinsky should not be thought of as a composer who used to provide sensation in a sensation-loving age, but as one whose merits will be plainly revealed to us as soon as we begin to seek the substance of truth, beauty and humour, and to scorn their shadow.

RAKHMANINOF

CHAPTER V

RAKHMANINOF

(1)

WITH the nationalist traditions of Russian music
the musical world is now tolerably familiar, and
the names of the symphonic and operatic works
inspired by them have become household words
among the musical nations. But whilst Western
Europe has been acquainting itself with the
beauties of *A Life for the Tsar, Antar, Tamara,
The Snow-Maiden* and *Boris Godounof*, there has
come into being another characteristic—one can
hardly call it a tradition—of the Russian musician,
and, if it is rarely paraded, the reason must be
that it passes unnoticed, having become an unfailing attribute of the representative composers
of the Russian School.

In the early days of the " New Russian " group,
when the leaders of musical thought were for the
most part " Sunday musicians "—a term applied
in friendly fashion by Liszt to Borodin—technical
proficiency was regarded, if not as a negligible
quantity, then, at any rate, as not indispensable,
and the accusation of "dilettantism" was a commonplace in the conversation of the professional,

155

and often reactionary, neo-classicist opponents of nationalism and progress alike. But when Rimsky-Korsakof, emerging from a long period of technical study, proved himself to have acquired a musicianship unrivalled at the time by any other musician in Russia, the reproach began to lose point, and Glazounof, his pupil, who succeeded him as the figure-head of Russian musical society, has earned for himself a universal respect as a thoroughly equipped musician, as worthy of his post at the head of the Petrograd Conservatoire as any occupant of such a position.

In Rakhmaninof, however, we find the quality of all-round musicianship developed in a degree apparently unexampled in Russian musical history. As a composer he possesses a technique which constitutes, like that of Medtner though in a somewhat less degree, an interest in itself ; his creative output is as varied as that of any of his compatriots ; as a conductor he has made a reputation for himself, both in the opera-house and the concert-room, which has fallen short of notoriety only because it has been earned solely by sheer interpretative ability and unswerving devotion to the composer's interests. It is on this account that his own remarkable pianistic gifts have attracted less attention than would have been the case had instrumental virtuosity been the principal sphere of his activities. The foundation of Rakhmaninof's reputation was laid by his creative work, and as his chief interest as a performer is that of interpretation it is as a composer that he is regarded by the public, even when seated at the piano. It is a well-deserved compliment.

In a musician whose destiny it has been to consolidate a tradition of musicianship introduced somewhat tardily as a feature of native musical activities, one hardly expects to find that desire for new modes of expression, for methods sought partly in the interests of musical progress and partly as a means of divesting the native product of every borrowed characteristic. But in recording that in Rakhmaninof's creative work there is a disposition to worship at the shrines of the early nineteenth-century romanticists, we are bound to acknowledge that his musical tastes have not been allowed to develop into prejudices. As a propagandist he has done work that, were it made known, would bring an added lustre to his fame.

That Rakhmaninof was for some years known to Western Europe and the New World as the composer of one attractive little piece can only now be regarded as a jest made by Dame Circumstance, and made with a full realization of its ultimate significance. That initial reputation has misled the continents, but Rakhmaninof is gradually living it down. On the day that his name attracts the remotest admirer of the cele-

brated *Prelude* to a performance of *The Niggardly
Knight*, Circumstance's possession of a sense of
humour will no longer be in any doubt.

(2)

Sergei Vassilievich Rakhmaninof was born on
March 20th, 1873, at Onega, in the Government
of Novgorod. The child was but four years of
age when his mother observed signs of a taste for
music, and she at once began to teach him the
piano, continuing to do so until he was nine, when
he was given into the care of a qualified lady-
pianist. To the guidance of these two women
Rakhmaninof owes the foundation of his serious
regard for the musical art.

When, in 1882, the family removed to Petrograd,
the boy at once entered the Conservatoire and
was placed in the piano class of Demyansky, his
theoretical studies being conducted by the then
recently appointed Professor L. A. Sacchetti,
subsequently famous for his musical erudition.
Circumstance decreed, however, that the Petrograd institution was not to have the sole credit of
educating the future master. In 1885, after three
years' tuition, the Rakhmaninof family were
obliged to migrate to Moscow, and thus it is with
the ancient capital and with its Conservatoire (and
to a great extent with the latter's traditions) that
the composer's name is identified. For a time he

took private lessons with Tchaikovsky's friend Zvieref, and, while living at the *pensionnat* conducted by this famous teacher, first made the acquaintance of Skryabin, with whom he at once became very friendly. Later he passed into the hands of Siloti, his cousin, who had formerly been a pupil of Zvieref, entering the classes of Taneyef and Arensky for theory and composition. Young Rakhmaninof, it seems, had no great love for the study of counterpoint, his disinclination being shared by Skryabin. Neither student cared much for Arensky, a professor whose attitude towards his charges was somewhat despotic, and in 1891, when Siloti, owing to a disagreement with Safonof, who had just been appointed director of the Conservatoire, resolved to sever his connection therewith, Rakhmaninof decided to leave as soon as possible. He contrived to signalize his departure in the following year in happy fashion by taking with him the large gold medal awarded for his one-act opera, *Aleko*, written to Nemirovich-Danchenko's version of Pushkin's *The Gipsies*.

The promise shown as a student began at once to be fulfilled. What is styled by a biographer, Rakhmaninof's " artistic baptism of fire " was undergone during the winter of 1892, when he made his first public appearance as a pianist at one of the concerts organized by Glavach in connection with the Moscow Electrical Exhibition then being held. In the following year the *Gipsy Dances* from *Aleko* were given a performance by Safonof. Gratified by this early success as a composer, he began to devote himself energetically to the creative side of his art. During 1893 he wrote a piano suite, the six songs (Opus 4), a suite for two pianos, two violin pieces, a further half-dozen songs (Opus 8), his first piano concerto, and the symphonic tableau, *The Rock*. Tchaikovsky's death in the autumn of this year inspired him to compose the fine *Elegiac Trio* now enjoying a belated esteem.

Meanwhile his reputation as a composer was steadily growing. *The Rock* was produced early in 1894, while the Trio was performed at one of his own concerts. A number of piano pieces, for two and four hands, and the *Gipsy Caprice* for orchestra were composed, the latter being given under Rakhmaninof's direction in 1895. Following up his success, he produced in turn his first symphony, conducted at one of the Russian Symphony Society's concerts at Petrograd by Glazounof in 1895, some choruses, piano pieces, and a goodly number of songs.

In September, 1897, there came an abrupt change in the sphere of his activities. Invited by S. I. Mamontof to undertake the conductorship of his reconstituted " Private " Opera, Rakhmaninof welcomed so splendid an opportunity of

RAKHMANINOF.

enlarging his experience. But before long he realized that the constant round of rehearsal and performance would necessitate a total renunciation of creative work, and, disenchanted, he relinquished his post after one season. In the year following his resignation he had reason to be thankful for the comparatively short though crowded term of office, for he was invited to London, where at a Philharmonic concert (1899) he was able to add the rôle of experienced conductor to those of pianist and composer, with which his name was already associated in the West. This journey proved to be the first of a series of visits to the leading musical centres of Europe.

These travels prolonged the period of creative inactivity. Towards the end of 1899, however, he resumed composing, and in the following spring conducted a work for voice and orchestra founded upon the " Fate " theme of Beethoven's fifth symphony. A second piano suite, a new concerto and a sonata for piano and 'cello soon followed, and were produced without delay. His activities were occasionally interrupted for the purpose of fulfilling engagements abroad, and finding himself in Vienna, in 1902, he resolved to visit Bayreuth ere returning home, with the object of obtaining a closer acquaintance with the music of Wagner and the approved method of producing the Wagnerian dramas.

Oddly enough, while apparently influenced by what he saw, his thoughts appear to have wandered in the homeward direction, and when subsequently turning his attention to the question of a reformed opera, chose the Russian, and narrower, path—that opened up by Dargomijsky's *The Stone Guest*—in preference to the broader road trodden by the German master. His declamatory one-act opera, *The Niggardly Knight*, was, like the "key-stone of the New Russian opera,"[1] composed to the original and unchanged text of Pushkin, and this work suitably completes the musical setting of the poet's three dramatic scenes, of which Rimsky-Korsakof's text for his *Mozart and Salieri* is the third.

A further work somewhat similar in style is *Francesca da Rimini*, on Modeste Tchaikovsky's libretto; here, however, Rakhmaninof's method approaches a little more closely to that of Wagner. Both these works were performed under the composer's direction in 1904, when he once again found himself occupying the conductor's chair, this time at the Great Theatre. This engagement lasted for two years, and was abruptly terminated owing to the presence of Rakhmaninof's name among the signatories of a petition for the autonomy of the Imperial Theatres, presented during the period

[1] The description applied by Cui to Dargomijsky's opera, *The Stone Guest*.

of political turmoil in 1906. He soon found
another sphere in which to make use of his experience as conductor, undertaking the direction
of the Society of Friends of Russian Music.

In 1907 he visited Paris for the Russian Festival
in company with Rimsky-Korsakof and Glazounof,
and there met his former fellow-student Skryabin,
recently returned from America. He conducted
his Cantata *Spring* and played the second piano
concerto.

In 1909 came Rakhmaninof's turn to make the
acquaintance of the New World, touring the
United States in the triple rôle of pianist, conductor and composer during that and the following
year. Despite the encouraging financial aspect
of this visit, Rakhmaninof expressed himself as
somewhat dissatisfied with a public which evidently measured the merit of an artist by the
number of his " recalls."

On returning to Russia he wrote the celebrated
symphonic suite inspired by Böcklin's picture *The
Island of Death* and the D minor piano sonata, and
in 1912 brought forward a Liturgy of St. John
Chrysostom for mixed chorus, a number of piano
preludes, and a third concerto. Following these
came a curious *pièce d'occasion* in the shape of the
Letter to Stanislavsky, written to commemorate
the latter's services as founder and manager of
the Moscow Art Theatre. On its production the

" letter " was sung by Shalyapin. During the season 1913-14 he produced his choral work, based on Edgar Allan Poe's *The Bells*.

Prior to the outbreak of war Rakhmaninof had been constantly engaged as conductor in both capitals, and as the various Russian musical enterprises have survived the vicissitudes through which they passed in the early days of the conflict his services have been much in demand. He has also interested himself in many good causes, has joined Kussevitsky in giving concerts in aid of war funds, and has shown great enthusiasm as an interpreter of his lamented comrade Skryabin. His recitals are a feature of Moscow musical life, and he is apparently the idol of Muscovite audiences.

(3)

As a symphonic writer Rakhmaninof is apparently content to take his instrument as he finds it. Like Glinka, he is not disposed to avail himself of " every modern luxury." His orchestral works are devoid of anything in the nature of a " tendency," and even in such a work as the second symphony (Opus 27), where he is evidently influenced by Tchaikovsky, and has produced music that fluctuates between the abstract and the introspective, he does not emulate the composer of " 1812 " either by piling up climaxes or by seeking new effects in the sphere of instrumentation.

Reviewing his orchestral works as a whole, one observes an inclination to cast off the allegiance to pure classicism and to strike out in the programmatic direction. The intention is shown in such examples as *The Rock* (Opus 7), written to a quatrain from Lermontof, and the *Island of Death* ; but the latter work certainly leaves an impression that if Rakhmaninof was impelled by a poetic inspiration to reproduce the content of the painter's canvas, his musical nature is not of a kind to help him adequately to express the feelings aroused by it through the medium he has chosen.

In reality, Rakhmaninof has attempted to go a little further towards musical programmaticism than the romanticists and has fallen between two platforms. A strongly poetic nature makes him disinclined to limit himself to the musical reflection of his own feelings, and he attempts the positively descriptive, which is certainly not his *métier*. He is less of a " pictorial " musician even than Glazounof, and would probably have given us something of greater significance had he confined himself to a form of orchestral composition in which, using a classical orchestra, he might have allowed full rein to his gift for polyphonic writing, for the creation of diverse rhythmic streams, for the composition of music that depends on its melodic, harmonic and contrapuntal interests.

How infinitely more at home he is when writing for the piano ! But here he is content to remain entirely conservative, and anything in the nature of novelty is indeed far to seek. As a composer for his own instrument he is relatively a classicist, for one cannot, in days when music is almost universally accepted as primarily a medium of expression, continue to reserve this category for the pre-Beethovenians, and in styling Rakhmaninof an old-fashioned romanticist, one has in mind a differentiation between the real modernist, who makes no apology for boldly attempting illustration by means of music, and the nineteenth-century romanticist of the Schumann or Chopin type who, from our point of view, is to be considered as having merely hinted, and sometimes a little faint-heartedly, at the emancipation of music and its enfranchisement as a highly expressive art.

In the smaller piano pieces, of which Rakhmaninof has composed a large number, he writes in a variety of moods and styles. At times he is meditative, as in the B major Prelude (No. 11) from the series Opus 32, on occasion almost feminine in delicacy, as in the fifth item of the same set ; although he rarely approaches the uncompromising "popularness" of the Polka, which forms part of the Album inaugurating the Russian Music Publishing Company's Edition, the G minor Prelude from the group of ten (Opus 23), dedicated to Siloti, is quite fairly to be described as a concession to those who prefer the lighter kind of music ; examples are to be found in which there is a greater ruggedness than in Brahms, though falling short of the rather savage emotionalism of Medtner ; sometimes he surpasses the lyricism of Schumann and is as tuneful as Mendelssohn. Then there are instances, too, of a leaning towards pure classicism, as in Nos. 3 and 8 of Opus 32, and in the sonata Opus 28 ; but his individuality is best shown in the works in which occur those heroic moments which his popular Prelude had led us to expect. It is in pieces of this kind, in the last bars of No. 13 of Opus 32, in the opening of the second of the three piano concertos, that he seems to be writing for himself, and when he is in this half-rhapsodic, half-heroic mood he sets a heavy task for pianists of less power and resource.

Rakhmaninof has made an important addition to the four-handed repertoire. The Fantasia, Opus 5, has four movements of a well-varied character representing the composer at his best in his first period ; in the second—using folk-material—he adopts a procedure rare enough with him. A further example entitled *Second Suite* consists of an Introduction, a Valse, a Romance and a Tarantella.

(4)

Rakhmaninof's reputation as a composer of concerted chamber-music, established in 1894 by his Elegiac Trio (Opus 9)—written in the previous year on the death of Tchaikovsky—still rests upon that work, for, excluding the piano sonata, which does not come under that heading, his only contribution to this class of musical literature is the sonata for 'cello and piano (Opus 19).

But the Trio, although dedicated "to the memory of a great artist," made a belated appearance in those parts of Western Europe in which the composer whom it commemorates has been for so long honoured, and it was not until 1912, some eighteen years after the production of the work in Moscow, that it was first brought to the notice of amateurs in this country by the Leeds Trio. In form the Trio resembles that which Tchaikovsky dedicated to the memory of another "great artist"—Nicholas, the brother of Anton Rubinstein. Opening with a Moderato movement, the second section consists of a theme and variations, while the Finale returns, like that of Tchaikovsky, to the thematic substance of the first movement. Possibly because of the delay in its first hearing, Rakhmaninof's work has not enjoyed the vogue accorded its predecessor, but for those able to consider the Trio in relation to the date of its composition, it is possible to understand the enthusiasm with which it was received in Russia.

Balancing the reticence of the composer in the region of concerted chamber-music, we observe in the vocal department an abundance, especially in solo-songs, that places Rakhmaninof among the many .prolific Russian composers for the voice. In quality his earlier essays were far below that of such vocal reformers as Moussorgsky, or inspired lyricists as Borodin, but with the increase in his output has come a signal improvement in manner. "Rakhmaninof's taste," says Cui, in *Russian Song*, "does not secure him against affected oddness, from a strangeness of modulation carried to the degree of downright ugliness ('A Prayer'); one meets with features that are unsuitable and illogical. . . . When Rakhmaninof discards elegance and affectation . . . when he perceives that in simplicity of speech can be expressed new thoughts and strong feelings, when he succeeds in maintaining throughout his songs the highest level of which he is capable, then will he produce examples which may well be pronounced irreproachable."

In the later songs there is certainly no affectation of strangeness. On the contrary, Rakhmaninof appears to have quickly become content with a beauty of a more or less conventional kind, and his accompaniments rarely essay the highly descriptive. Occasionally one observes a novel touch, as in the concluding bars of " Christ is Risen " (Opus 26, No. 6) and " Sorrow in Spring-time " (Opus 21, No. 12), but he has preferred to write music, when setting a text for vocal purposes, that is more in the nature of an accompaniment to his vocal line than a complement or amplification of the poet's words. Generally speaking, Rakhmaninof is at his best in songs where the piano part is of a light texture, such, for instance, as " Night is mournful " (Opus 26, No. 12) and the very charming " Lilacs," but he is also to be credited with examples in which a wealth of sound has contributed to the beauty of the song, and, at the same time, to the descriptiveness of the whole ; " Spring Waters " (Opus 14, No. 11) provides an instance of this, the climactic moment at the words " Spring is here," when the earlier arpeggio figure is repeated in heavy chords, successfully reproduces the sentiment of the text, which is altogether very happily translated into music. Another song of which the same may be said is " How fair this spot " (Opus 21, No. 7), marred, however, by a somewhat commonplace conclusion. Such songs as the queer " Fate " (Opus 21, No. 1), in which the composer has set

Apoukhtin's words to music, embodying the
well-known Beethovenian theme, and the Khomiakof number "To the Children" (Opus 26,
No. 7), might well lead one to suppose that
Rakhmaninof could never again restrict himself
to the conventional type of lyric, but the trite
accompaniment of the baritone song, "When
yesterday we met" (Opus 26, No. 13), effectively
disposes of this supposition. On the whole,
Rakhmaninof's songs exhibit no striking harmonic
novelty and no startling formal innovations; they
have certain sterling qualities, and, at times, a
few defects that are not the outcome of over-
daring poetic ambitions. He is no realist; his
songs are always pleasing, nearly always dignified,
but never profoundly moving.

In his choral works Rakhmaninof has been
accused of an originality not directly relating to
their musical essence. He appears to have met
with a certain reluctance on the part of choruses
to undertake the performance of music which
demanded a revision of views as to what is
"vocal"; this circumstance recalls the reception
of Sir Edward Elgar's *Dream of Gerontius* which,
it will be remembered, caused some perturbation
in choral circles. In the Liturgy of St. John
Chrysostom, produced in 1910 by the Moscow
Synodal Choir, he showed no disposition to compromise with the objectors; moreover, he incurred

criticism on a different score, for it was alleged that the Liturgy was of too " free " a style to be considered properly sacred. It is pronounced, however, apart from the features which prevent its adoption by the Orthodox Church, to possess a spirituality at least the equal of that of any other example of Russian music of its class. In accordance with the decree excluding instrumental music from the Russian Church, these works are, of course, *a capella*. It is by the work for chorus and orchestra, entitled *Spring*, written to a text by Nekrassof, that Rakhmaninof is best known as a choral composer in Western Europe. It has an important part for baritone solo which has been the means, through Shalyapin's interpretation, of spreading knowledge of the composition.

Of late the composer has devoted himself somewhat freely to devotional music, and a series of twelve anthems on early Church themes has become highly popular in Russia, but the setting of Balmont's version of *The Bells*—the projected performance of which, at Sheffield in the autumn of 1914, was prevented by the war—proves that he does not intend to quit the domain of secular choral music.

(5)

It seems strange that while a painter can himself decide by what work he is to be represented in a country in which he has hitherto been unknown, a composer has not always a voice in the selection. Thus Rakhmaninof's reputation as an operatic composer rests for us—and it is said, much to his regret—on the early diploma work, *Aleko*, a composition which he probably regards as an historical document relating to the meteoric appearance of Mascagni's *Cavalleria Rusticana*, by which it is influenced. *Aleko* is founded on Pushkin's celebrated poem *The Gipsies*, reproduced in a dramatic version by Nemirovich-Danchenko. The plot relates to the choice of a gipsy life and wife by a man weary of the world. His experience of the Romanies is unfortunate, and when he discovers how lightly his Zemfira regards her marriage vows, he stabs her and her lover too. To this rather slender material Rakhmaninof has wedded music that interests one very little more than the drama of which it is the complement. The vocal line of the opera is melo-declamatory, but there are certain concessions to popular taste in the direction of verbal repetition, and an occasional melodic turn vaguely suggesting the idiosyncrasies of gipsy-song. The short *Intermezzo* makes no attempt to imitate Mascagni's, either in manner or matter, and it is clear that it was not written with the idea of courting comparison ; but the gipsy dances, constituting the *divertissement* of the opera, have secured a popularity that has brought them into the programme of Russian Ballet schemes in which they form an attractive feature. *Aleko* was revived in 1903 at the Imperial Theatre, Moscow, when Shalyapin undertook the part of the old gipsy, Aleko's father-in-law.

Cheshikin speaks of *Aleko* as being a work of promise. But the prophesied fulfilment has but a remote relationship with that first operatic essay.

When, after fourteen years' interval, Rakhmaninof turned his attention once again to the stage, he chose a path on which few can ever have expected him to step.

In the later 'nineties Rimsky-Korsakof elected to pay a tribute to Dargomijsky, and to that end set Pushkin's *Mozart and Salieri*, one of the three dramatic scenes of which *The Stone Guest* is the first, without changing the original text. A few years afterwards Rakhmaninof took the remaining work, *The Niggardly Knight*, retaining also the unaltered text, and writing music of a purely melo-declamatory kind. The result is something which surpasses *The Stone Guest* in austerity, partly because it is not relieved by the incidental, though quite legitimate, lyrics of Dargomijsky's work, and partly owing to the conspicuous lack of dramatic movement in the text. Probably, in writing music to such a " plot " as is afforded by the behaviour of an avaricious Baron, who vilifies his only son rather than yield to him a single piece of his miserly hoard, Rakhmaninof had no other intention than the emulation of the composer of *The Stone Guest* or the completion of the musical setting of Pushkin's three miniature dramas. Still, there is a good deal of interest in the score, since Rakhmaninof has succeeded in following, though somewhat vaguely, the general dramatic trend of the text. There are leading-motives which are well chosen, that of the vigorous Albert being well adapted for the suggestion of a knightly character, while those of the Jew and the skinflint Baron are sufficiently diversified. The principal fault of the opera, which has no feminine characters, lies in the too-persistent use of these leading-motives; had they been made to give way to a more detailed musical reference to the text instead of monopolizing the orchestra with a continuous and redundant description of the character who happens to be speaking, *The Niggardly Knight* would have possessed a quality more significant than that constituted by its conformity in structure to the mentioned works of its kind.

A further opera, presented on the same evening as *The Niggardly Knight* at the Great Theatre, Moscow, in 1913, is *Francesca da Rimini*, written to Modeste Tchaikovsky's version of that portion of Dante's *Inferno* used by his brother as the literary basis of a well-known orchestral work. *Francesca da Rimini* consists of two tableaux joined by an Intermezzo, a Prologue and an Epilogue. The principal singing characters are Virgil's Shade, Dante, Lanceotto, Paolo and Francesca, a soprano. The chorus of spectres sing no words, but express their sentiments by means of an undulating vocal line sung at times with closed lips, at others on the syllable "Ah." The solo-parts are consistently declamatory, and the orchestral music partakes of the nature of a long symphonic picture, being quite un-"operatic." Its harmony and figuration often recall Wagner, particularly in the duet between the two principal characters in the second tableau, which contains some of the most pleasing music of the opera.

Francesca da Rimini must be looked upon as a daring experiment ; the boldness does not lie in its harmonies but in the implication that at some future time the opera-going public will be content with a form of music-drama in which the drama is virtually negligible, and of which the music, though beautiful, contains but a faint suggestion of the emotions experienced by the *dramatis personæ*.

REBIKOF

CHAPTER VI

REBIKOF

(1)

IT is no new experience to find coupled with the name of a composer an expressed intention of initiating reforms. Gluck, Wagner and Dargomijsky concerned themselves with an opera which had become effete and meaningless. Glinka and Liszt rebelled against the tyranny of the traditional symphonic mould. Concerted chamber-music, the quartet in particular, has been freed from the cramping convention of sonata-form, in which it was at one time thought that all music of this class must be patterned. The long and strenuously opposed idea of pictorial music has gained acceptance, and at certain vital moments in social history the world is inclined to look upon " absolute " music as something less than what music can and, indeed, ought to be.

But, unfortunately, while reformers in one sphere or another of music do from time to time arise, the avowed prophet of music as the language of the emotions is a rare bird. One supposes that every inspired composer reflects his innermost feelings when in the act of musical creation, but he does not bear in mind that although the traditional harmonic language in which they are expressed is, as it were, second nature to him, its formal shape has, in reality, only an accidental relation to those feelings, the accident in question being constituted by his musical training and his experience of stereotyped musical formulas.

In Rebikof we have a trained musician who proposes to avail himself, to a certain extent, of his education, so far as concerns harmony, but to ignore formal restrictions not only in the sphere of architectonics, but in that of harmony itself. Rebikof has formulated a definite creed ; it was communicated to the Editor of the Russian edition of Riemann's *Dictionary of Music*, and is quoted in part in Cheshikin's *The Russian Opera*. "Music," he says, "is the language of our emotions ; our emotions have neither form nor defined limits ; their expression in music should, therefore, conform to this condition."

To one of his compositions, however, he prefixes a quotation from Tolstoi's provocative essay, *What is Art ?* choosing by this means to elucidate the message of his creed. At the head of his *Musico-Psychological Tableau*, entitled *Bondage and Liberty*, stands the following excerpt from the above-mentioned volume : ". . . And it is to be considered art, also, when a person, having experienced or imagined feelings of gladness, joy, grief, despair, courage, melancholy, and the transition from one of these feelings to another, has expressed such feelings by means of sounds so that the listener has been infeeted by or has experienced them just as he has experienced them." Having perused and digested this borrowed exposition, we are prepared for the following : " I conceive the funetion of music to be the transmission of emotions and moods, but not ideas, for the expression of which we have *words*. Our feelings have *neither forms nor cadences*." So much for theory. We shall presently consider its application by Rebikof.

(2)

With regard to the date of Vladimir Ivanovich Rebikof's birth, all authorities, excepting the composer himself, agree. He was born, says Cheshikin, on May 19th, 1866, at Krasnoyarsk, in Siberia. Since it is reasonable to suppose that a jubilee article in honour of the fiftieth anniversary of " the father of Russian Modernism," which appeared in May, 1916, must have been challenged had it been an anachronism, we are presumably safe in attributing the statement furnished by Rebikof for Ivanof's *History of Musical Development in Russia* to a lapse of memory. It begins with the information that he

first saw the light in 1867. ". . . I was taken,"
it continues, " when quite a child, to Moscow
by my parents. I studied in the Modern School
there, and completed my course. After this I
decided to devote myself to music, and with this
aim began lessons in theory with Klenovsky."
Rebikof says nothing further of his general education, and upon this Ivanof, a thorough-going
reactionary and showing a marked partiality for
Eclecticism, bases the odd conjecture that the
composer's early departure for Berlin was taken
at an age at which he was too susceptible to foreign
influences. Whether this is intended to refer to
the theoretical instruction received from Meyer-
berger, or to the piano lessons of Müller, does not
transpire. Following these studies Rebikof proceeded to Vienna, where he became a pupil of
Jaksch, in instrumentation. It seems likely that
the choice of Schnitzler's *The Lady with the
Dagger* may have originated in tastes formed whilst
in the Austrian capital.

In the biographical narrative above referred to
Rebikof gives no account of his movements from
the time of his initial studies with Jaksch until
1894, when he appears to have been already
established for some time in Odessa, sufficiently
long, at all events, to gain the ear of the local
Opera directorate. In this year was here produced
his first dramatic work, *The Storm* (after Koro-

lenko), written before the composer had thrown off the influence—very marked in his early compositions—of Tchaikovsky. The Odessa public, notorious to this day for its lack of sound musical taste, did not take kindly to *The Storm*, but Rebikof does not seem to have been discouraged ; remaining in Odessa for a further four years, he founded a branch of the Society of Composers with the aim of carrying on a propaganda on behalf of native musicians, and also for the purpose of collecting fees accruing from the performance of their works. " I perceived, however," says the organizer, " that this idea did not meet with sufficient sympathy," but he omits to say whether the composers or the performers were unsympathetic !

Following the initial performance of *The Storm*, this two-act opera was produced more successfully at Jitomir ; the comparative warmth of its reception may possibly be due to the local associations with Korolenko, its original author, who was born there in 1853. It was next mounted at Kishinef, where Rebikof again found musical life at a rather low ebb. Possibly it was on this account that he chose that town as the new centre of his activities. He began in 1898 by opening a local branch of the Imperial Russian Musical Society, attaching to its industries the conduct of musical classes, and soon these grew into a regular school of music. During the sojourn at Kishinef he composed the well-known *Christmas Tree*. He had at this date already begun to experiment with the whole-tone scale, and henceforth his compositions were to be generously coloured by the harmonies founded thereon.

In 1901 he migrated to Moscow and, abandoning, his tutorial work, established himself as a teacher in the wider sense—addressing the greater public by means of his compositions and newspaper articles. *The Christmas Tree* and *The Storm* were produced at the Aquarium Theatre, Moscow, in October, 1903. " For the sensitive artist," wrote Krouglikof, "*The Christmas Tree* is a revelation ; for the musician, it is full of interest ; for the pedant, an outrageous affront." The work has, however, outlived its original strangeness and is congenial to all but the most conservative, partly, perhaps, because its composer has since contrived to give us something more consistently strange, music without lapses into the positively commonplace such as are to be found in *The Christmas Tree*. Since this date Rebikof has laboured energetically to re-establish music as the " language of the emotions " by means both of precept and practice. His more recent dramatic works are *Thea*, a *Musico-Psychological Drama* in four tableaux, a *Musico-Psychological Tale* founded on Andreyef's story, *The Abyss*, the music of which was written in Prague in 1907, *Alpha and Omega*, which is in the same category as *Thea* but with only two tableaux (composed in 1911). He has also published a number of sacred compositions which include a Liturgy of St. John Chrysostom. Among his literary labours are a number of articles contributed to the *Russian Musical Gazette* and a Russian version of Gevaert's *Orchestration*, with additional illustrations from native composers. In his articles he reveals himself as a " musical protestant," desiring not so much an acceptation of the inevitability of musical evolution as a return to the primitive psychological function of the art. In his music he has certainly been a pioneer, but he must be taxed with having over-emphasized certain unessential innovations. If it is his intention " to shock the middle-class " or its easily recognizable equivalent in the musical world, he may undoubtedly claim success ; but seeing that his critical and exegetical writings bear the stamp of sincerity, it is a great pity that he does not succeed in prevailing upon some of his champions to prosecute their advocacy with a little more discretion and perhaps a little less zeal. His dramatic works and essays in dramatic form have brought him a considerable attention on the part of musicians, due in some cases to the originality of their form and in others to the evident catholicity of the composer's literary taste; his piano pieces are of an accessible kind and have found their way into the curriculum, and his songs are popular with concert givers and goers.

Rebikof should be content with a reputation as pioneer, protestant or purist (he has been compared in that quality with Moussorgsky), and with the popularity he has earned among music-lovers who, without knowledge of his ideals, are grateful for his music. But to claim genius for this composer is to place rather too high a value upon what after all is only success in experiment.

(3)

When we examine the manner in which Rebikof applies his theories in actual composition, we experience a feeling of disappointment. Rebikof has in some quarters been hailed as a follower of Moussorgsky. But the composer of *Boris Godounof* did rather more than ask that music should be a spontaneous expression of feelings ; he wrote spontaneously. Rebikof, on the contrary, a professing purist, is a scientist directly he puts pen to paper. Deprecating all forms he invents new ones ; vowing that music shall henceforth be free to mirror the emotions, he names his chords and only falls short of complete perversity by failing to attach these chords systematically to a particu-

lar emotion or sentiment. He claims to have
attempted to re-establish music as the language
of the emotions ; he implies that music should
begin where words fail ; but in reality he has
busied himself in coining musical words. " These
chords," he proclaims, in one of his most recent
works, " are to be found in my earlier writings,"
and he furnishes a detailed list of their former
lodgings. The harmonies thus specified are the
equivalent of words or verbal expressions, and as
they have been used indiscriminately in works of
such entirely different nature as *The Christmas
Tree*, which contains certain supernatural material,
and in *The Abyss*, an ultra-realistic setting of
Andreyef's horrible story, and in such "absolute"
music as the *Feuille d'Album* and the Dances
(Opus 51), one is obliged to conclude either that
they are meaningless, or that the composer's
emotions are strictly limited in kind—that he is
affected similarly by the contemplation of dire
physical necessity or by that of an acute appetite
for intellectual sympathy.

What are the forms into which Rebikof chooses
to pour the material which is represented as giving
expression to his emotions ? In the music of
the *Melomimics* (Opus 11) we observe that the
Tchaikovskian manner of the *Rêveries d'Automne*
is being thrown off and that the search for a new
path has begun. But the composer claims novelty

in respect of the mould itself. A " Melomimic,"
he informs us, " is a kind of scenic art in which
mimicry and instrumental music are blended in
an indivisible whole. The Melomimic differs
from the Ballet in that dances do not play in it
any part at all; from pantomime, in that music
plays in it a rôle not less important than mimicry. The region of mimicry begins where words
end and where emotion reigns alone." The
literary material on which the three Melomimics (Opus 11) are based is drawn from N.
Wagner's fairy-tale *Milla and Nolli*. Three
episodes are depicted, and, as the movements of
the protagonists and their emotions are described
in the music without the suggestive dances of the
ballet, the Melomimic appears to resolve itself
into a miniature wordless play.

In the *Vocal Scenes* we have a more distinctive form. Here are instrumental music,
vocal and pantomime. There is one vocal part
and one played in gesture, the literary foundation consisting of poems by such as Brioussof
and Apukhtin.

The *Melodeclamations* are miniatures in which
poetry has been set to music that follows the accents of the verse; the voice has, however, a
rhythmic and not a melodic articulation. The
Melodeclamations, Opus 32, are written to
poems of Heine and Apukhtin.

The *Musico-Psychological Tableau* would be better described as an instrumental tone-poem. *Bondage and Liberty* has, for instance, a title but no avowed " programme " ; the title implies a record of emotional movements, but no definite clue to their origin is afforded.

(4)

The qualification " psychological " again enters into the description of the dramatic works, all of them slight as to bulk. *The Christmas Tree*, a *Musico-Psychological Drama* which derives its title from Dostoyevsky, its supernatural element from Andersen, and its delivery in dramatic form from Hauptmann's Dream-Poem *Hannele*, has only two singing characters, one mimic and a number of supernumeraries. It consists of four tableaux, the second of which, doing duty as a ballet, represents the beggar-child's vision of the Christmas Tree. The commonplace *Valse Lente*, the *Procession of Gnomes*, the *Dance of Mummers* and the *Dance of Chinese Dolls*, the last-mentioned constructed on the Indo-Japanese pentatonic scale, are often used as a concert-suite. The music, apart from these instrumental numbers, becomes interesting when it is known that it created at one time a profound impression. Cheshikin, evidently somewhat disturbed at what this portends for the future of opera, speaks of an abundance of consecutive fifths, and appears to be horrified that the work concludes on an augmented triad. He attributes Rebikof's repudiation of the key-signature to Dargomijsky's influence (*Stone Guest*), but fails to observe the series of complete tonal scales at the opening of the third tableau, a device which, having already been employed by Glinka and the composer of *The Stone Guest*, could hardly be claimed by Rebikof or his friends as an invention.

This music, at one time regarded as aggressively modern, is, in fact, beginning to date; it savours of the Italian " verists " and the French " impressionists," and on the whole gives an impression of faded sentimentality.

The Abyss (a *Musico-Psychological Tale*) is a work of quite a different order. It is little more than the composer's record of the conversation between Nemovetsky the student and Zinochka the school-girl, but the little more is sufficiently suggestive of the horrors of Andreyef's original to make one thankful that Rebikof has elected to ignore its essential or crucial material. As for its music, it is conceivable that in 1907, the date of its composition, *The Abyss* may have caused as great a consternation as had Andreyef's work previously, and what Tolstoi, whose wife was one of its author's assailants, would have thought of the composer's effort can be guessed with tolerable ease. For the musician it is to be described as an experiment in the conduct of consecutive fourths and fifths, the moments of ecstasy evoking chords consisting of five super-imposed fourths, a number increased in a subsequent work.

Rebikof's next dramatic undertaking is also placed in the category of *Musico-Psychological.* It is entitled *Alpha and Omega* and consists of two tableaux dealing with the appearance of Man on earth, and his transactions with Lucifer. The text is by the composer, who shows here that his indebtedness to Andreyef has been increased since the setting of *The Abyss* to music.

The music to *Alpha and Omega* is somewhat monotonous. It shows a considerable advance in harmonic style on that of *Thea*—an earlier example of the psychological music-drama which is Wagnerian in manner—being apparently influenced by *Death and Transfiguration.* But apart from an attempt at the characterization of the three principal figures, Man, Woman and Lucifer, *Alpha and Omega* contains in its few pages little that is likely to atone for its slender dramatic interest.

Not the least interesting of Rebikof's works for the theatre are the dramatized versions of Krilof's fables. The composer has selected ten numbers from the collection left by the Russian La Fontaine, has arranged them for the stage and has set them to appropriate music. The dramatic arrangement is curious, and, unfortunately, a little difficult. On the rise of the curtain, Krilof is seen sitting at his writing table engaged in penning his celebrated fables. At the beginning of each number the Fabulist raises his head and declaims the title and the opening words. The back-cloth is drawn and the scenic setting of the fable disclosed. During the action Krilof is occupied in writing the fable represented to the audience. At the close of each, the back-cloth or wall of Krilof's room is used to screen the scenic change. The numbers that must prove of greatest interest to musicians are those of the *Funeral* and *The Quartet*. The first introduces the conventionalized Oriental idiom as accompaniment of the professional keeners or wailing-women, who are so greedy for corpses that they welcome a proposed quickening of the dead, having first obtained a promise that a second death shall follow ! The second depicts the futile efforts of four animals to obtain a satisfactory instrumental *ensemble*. Rebikof, still a firm believer in his terminology, calls his version " Musico-psychological satires."

(5)

What is the music that Rebikof has poured into these moulds ? Of what does this added psychological element consist ? So far as one can see,

REBIKOF.

the composer's technical development is the one
important thing recorded in them. His principal
works, reviewed as music, appear to represent
steps or stages in the evolution or development of
a system of harmony. Thus we have the *Rêveries
d'Automne* as a sample of the primitive Rebikof,
aping Tchaikovsky; the *Rêves* (Opus 15), showing
him at the tonal-scale or Debussian stage; *The
Christmas Tree* (Opus 21), in which he seems to
fall between these two ; the *Bondage and Liberty*
(Opus 22), which proclaims that he has emancipated himself from his slavery to the tonal-scale
only to fall under the yoke of Strauss. In the
Melodeclamations, the composer steps back as
though better to leap—into *The Abyss*, in which
he offers a curious mixture of the French (Conservatoire) idiom and Skryabinisms. After this
the *Chansons Blanches*, wherein, exploiting fourths,
Rebikof selects as his material a by-product of the
process by which Skryabin has extracted gold
from ore (neither psychology nor music as a
language is mentioned in this instance) ; later
the series of *Trois Idylles*, suggesting both by its
cover and its internal appearance and content,
that Rebikof can no longer hide the indebtedness
of the previous *Chansons Blanches* to Erik Satie,
and, finally, *Les Danses* (Opus 51), in which he
reaches already anticipated heights by piling upon
his harmonic Ossa a further interval of a fourth.

(6)

What, one asks, has all this to do with the vaunted language of the emotions ? How can Rebikof reconcile his contention that music should begin where words end with his preoccupation with these musical words—for that is the only term by which his carefully labelled devices can be described. No sooner does the composer strike a new chord than he proceeds to experiment with it, instead of choosing, as one would expect, to avert his gaze from its technical significance. When, for instance, as in Opus 14 (The Ballet Suite), he first reaches a harmony derived from the tonal scale, he behaves as though the resultant chord were charged with a strong electric current ; he is powerless to let go. The effect is in consequence altogether devoid of the kaleidoscopic quality one would, and is entitled to, expect in a Fairies' Dance.

Apparently Rebikof has no desire to repudiate this reputation as a pioneer. But the more closely we examine his product the more clearly is he shown to be a musician who has fallen under the sway of a succession of influences, the more evident it is that whilst thus influenced he confines his attention to their physical and not their poetical aspect. He may have been influenced at one time by Moussorgsky, but from that master he differs in that he is a persistent technician or mechanician ; between Debussy and Rebikof there is nothing in common beyond the use of the tonal scale, which for the former is a genuine expression of his musical individuality, but for the latter merely a technical expedient. As for the difference between the Russian and Satie, it may be said to consist in that the Frenchman smiles benignly at his weird experiments, whilst Rebikof is so desperately in earnest that he is in no mood to contemplate himself through the spectacles of criticism. When, however, they are donned by another, this industrious explorer in discovered territories appears in a very unfavourable light. His discoveries are none of them essential in themselves, and their novelty, moreover, is but comparative. His experiments are carried out and his expedients applied in a manner that fails to secure conviction.

So as to avoid distracting the attention of the audience from the music—which, be it remembered, is an expression of the emotions—he plays, we are told, behind a curtain. But should not the music itself, especially if it expresses emotions, provide a curtain ? The right-hand chords in the *Hymn to the Sun* (*Idylles*, Opus 50) are to be played with the side of the palm. Is it really worth while to acquire this palmar technique when the chords can quite well be played with the fingers ?

Even the suggested influence of pictures, such as is met with in certain places, and for which the composer vouches, appears to be in the nature of an affectation, and a not altogether harmless one! He tells us that he has been influenced by certain painters. In a footnote to one of the Dreams (Melomimics, Opus 15) we read that it is the composer's intention that the Demon should resemble the "Lucifer" of Franz Stuck's picture. The scenic instructions printed in the score of *Thea* direct that the stage decoration should be in the style of Böcklin. But of what importance are such indications when they come from a composer who has allowed the insertion of the appallingly mawkish frontispiece—in the style of the cheapest of chocolate boxes—in the score of *The Christmas Tree?*

It would be quite feasible for a man who had no musical taste or experience to divine that music ought to be free, and even though himself restricted to what de Quincey called "the infirmities" of verbal explanation, might succeed in convincing by argument. Having listened to him one would perhaps be willing to await with confidence the advent of an articulate musical genius, one capable of vindicating the theories advanced by his musically mute precursor.

That Rebikof the musician does not fulfil the promises of Rebikof the theorist is apparently due in some measure to his want of detachment, to his inability to dispel the consciousness of a technique. But the ephemeral quality of his music and its inadequacy as a fulfilment of his theories are surely attributable to the circumstance that he is too much of a musician and not enough of an artist.

TANEYEF

CHAPTER VII

TANEYEF

(1)

THE position of Taneyef in the world of Russian Music is in some respects similar to that of Glazounof. To the Muscovite also, fell part of the task of strengthening the fibre of this rapid growth. To ensure the welfare of its constitution in the future he dug deeply, seeking in the very roots of his art the secret of its evolution.

That he could not view altogether sympathetically the trend of modern music is clear from the record of his conversations, late in life, with Skryabin, but he was fully cognizant of the need of progress in music, and knew well that his teaching would assist in furthering it. If he did little as a composer to indicate on what lines the art of the future would proceed, he performed prodigies in another province, in securing a means of developing it. Taneyef was a great teacher, a fine scholar, a highly capable administrator and a most lovable man.

We have direct documentary evidence of his attitude towards the question of musical instruction. The *Manual of Counterpoint*, a voluminous work, on which he laboured for twenty years or so, may be looked upon as the ideal corrective for the "dilettantism" of the nationalist group, a carelessness which was instrumental in inspiring Taneyef's early detestation of the "mighty little heap," and of which, in his view, Moussorgsky was the embodiment. The *Manual* is the gospel of, "Thorough" in musical education. Its equivalent is perhaps to be found in the elaborate compilation of Sevčik, the father of modern fiddling. Each is a synthesis of mechanisms designed to secure a perfect technical fulfilment of the interpretative function.

In his bulky volume Taneyef has aimed at recording every possible species of contrapuntal combination, and, as though to leave no shadow of doubt as to his real intention, he furnishes his student with a contrivance not unlike the mechanic's "slide-rule," on which, when its working is understood, the intending composer may place the fullest reliance, and if he finds the process of acquiring the science of counterpoint a little arduous, he may rest assured that its application may be undertaken "without tears."

But Taneyef, despite the academic dryness discoverable in some of his own works, had not the intention of converting composition into an exact science, an application of his system as the fundament of a carefully calculated process. The means of his system is mathematical in kind, but the end at which it aims is that of creative facility. He desired to build up for the use of composers of the future a huge but mobile instrument, which would respond to every note of the composer's emotional nature. It was his conviction that counterpoint must cease to be regarded as a species of dead language, as an ancient literature, that it must form a vital element of all music. It was apparently the recognition of this fundamental truth that brought about the *rapprochement* between the Moscow theorist and Rimsky-Korsakof. The latter's studies, undertaken with the object of obtaining facility in expressing his poetic thoughts in music, gained Taneyef's sympathetic interest, and Rimsky-Korsakof, whose recently acquired mastery had aroused the envy of Tchaikovsky, avowed that in the presence of the latter's pupil he felt but a tyro.

It should not be imagined that the attitude of the author of the celebrated *Manual of Counterpoint* towards his pupils was despotic; his aim was that a pupil's individuality should be given an efficient vehicle of expression. "Above all," says Youry Engel, in a reminiscence of his student days, "Taneyef opened his pupils' eyes to the historical stages in the evolution of music, to the indispensability of a practical mastery of all the fundamental forms of this evolution, to the imperishable musical treasures of the past, and, in particular, to the half-forgotten epochs of contrapuntal polyphony, which still awaits its fručtifying renascence. His teaching of counterpoint, fugue and form obliged pupils to experience, as it were, on their own account, all the historical processes of musical evolution; he taught them to separate the essential from the accessory, to value the power, beauty and permanency of the classics . . . His class was a magnificent school of creative technique . . ."

Taneyef's personality must have counted for a good deal in his teaching. His kindly nature is reflečted in the many stories told about him, particularly in those referring to his affečtion for his old nurse, with whom he lived for several years, and who took the greatest interest in his work. Until forty years of age Taneyef shared with his brother the family home, but during the composition of his opera, *Orestes,* he sought a more secluded habitation, and, taking rooms, was looked after by this devoted old woman, who predeceased him by some four years. On her death in 1910, he dedicated a set of songs to her memory.

He inherited from his father a healthy appetite for general culture. He was a good linguist, fond of pičtures, and had a passion for rare books and manuscripts, of which he acquired a large number. But he was not a mere lover of costly bindings ;

his knowledge of literature was exceedingly wide, and ranged from Plato's Dialogues to the poetry of Balmont. His interest in social and intellectual questions was informed by his acquaintance with the great philosophers of the past; towards modern systems of philosophy his attitude was, we are told, one of caution. We have coupled the name of Taneyef with that of Glazounof, and as concerns Russian music—at a moment when a strong pedagogical influence came as a blessing, though to some disguised—the work of the two teachers has much in common; but our subject's attitude towards life and art finds a closer parallel in that of Joachim. A steadfast idealist, the purity of his work was never endangered; his purpose was lofty and his aim was single. What he undertook was faithfully performed, and that his labours in a good cause were generally acknowledged was not because he sought recognition. In the history of Russian Music there are many fascinating biographical stories; that of Taneyef is the record of a noble life.

(2)

Sergei Ivanovich Taneyef was born on November 13th, 1856. His father, a landowner, was distinguished both for his scholarship and his love of music. We have testimony to his general artistic culture in the record that he concluded an industrious university career by writing a dissertation on Tragedy, and that he was a tolerably good performer on both piano and violin. His son's early taste for literature and music did not therefore appear unexpectedly, and it was cultivated without difficulty and in natural fashion thanks to the immediate home influence and that of the many literary folk who foregathered from time to time at the Taneyefs'. The child's first musical instruction was received from a lady, Miropolsky by name, who gave him piano lessons. She was deeply impressed by the talent her pupil displayed and the industry with which he applied himself to his studies, and when the parents appeared willing that he should continue his musical education on a more generous scale, she took young Sergei, now ten years old, to call on Nicholas Rubinstein, the director of the Moscow Conservatoire. The latter was immediately convinced that the lad possessed gifts much above the average, and consented, despite his tender age, to take him under his care. Studying piano and theory with E. L. Langer, young Taneyef made so much progress that he soon attracted the attention of the staff and of his fellow-pupils. About a year after his entry he took part in a Students' Evening, playing a movement from one of Mozart's sonatas. Apparently he was at this time insufficiently endowed with self-confidence, for, mistaking for sarcasm the cordial manifestations of approval from the professors present, he burst into tears.

For the purposes of general education he was now sent to school; for two years his musical studies were to have been a secondary consideration. During 1869, however, Nicholas Rubinstein came to the conclusion that the gifted young fellow would be justified in embracing a musical career, given a due attention to the requisite training. He accordingly sent for the father, and, informing the latter that he hoped shortly to add general educational classes to the curriculum of the Conservatoire, induced the anxious parent to allow the lad to leave school and to devote himself more closely to music. In September of that year the complete course was entered upon, and the fully-fledged student began a four-years' piano course with the Director, taking theory lessons with N. G. Hubert, and harmony, instrumentation and free composition with Tchaikovsky, founding a friendship which lasted until the latter's death. He was also influenced to a considerable extent by some articles written by Laroche, which were instrumental in generating his profound affection for the classics.

At the end of six years the instruction he had received from these men, together with a native enthusiasm, had made of him an accomplished musician, and the Conservatoire acknowledged the qualities evinced by its *alumnus* by awarding him the large gold medal. On January 19th, 1875, Taneyef made his first public appearance, playing Brahms' D minor piano concerto and a couple of far less austere pieces by Chopin and Liszt. His success, endorsed by a eulogistic notice written by Tchaikovsky, brought him immediate recognition, and he was at once invited to visit a number of provincial towns in the capacity of soloist. A few months after his debut he received a further tribute from Tchaikovsky, whose B flat minor concerto, now universally known, he first introduced to the public. Another tour followed, in company with Auer, the violinist, at the conclusion of which he went abroad with Nicholas Rubinstein, visiting Turkey, Greece, and Italy, and, reaching Paris, stayed there for about a year. Here he entered fully into musical and intellectual life, meeting among many well-known Frenchmen, Gounod, Saint-Saens, Fauré, d'Indy and such distinguished compatriots as Turgenef and Saltikof, the satirist. On his return to Russia he made a concert tour of the Baltic provinces, settling down at its conclusion to a long period of pedagogic activity at the Moscow Conservatoire, to which he was invited in the first instance as Tchaikovsky's deputy.

TANEYEF.

Taneyef

On the death of Nicholas Rubinstein, in March,
1881, Hubert succeeded to his post, and Taneyef
took over the deceased director's piano-class,
retaining his theory and free-composition pupils.
This work he found too heavy, and it was for the
purpose of relieving the burden that Arensky was
invited to join the staff. But with Rubinstein's
guiding hand withdrawn, affairs within the Conservatoire began to assume an aspect less favour-
able. The new Director only remained a few
months in office, and the control was then vested
in an Inspectorship entrusted to Albrecht, who
was supported by a committee. Before long,
however, it was seen that a man possessing the
qualities of a musician and of an administrator was
needed, and in 1885, at Tchaikovsky's instance,
his former pupil was prevailed upon to accept the
Directorship. From that time on, thanks to his
labour and devotion, matters steadily improved,
and at the end of four years, when Taneyef
retired in order to occupy himself with composition, the Conservatoire had been established on a
basis firmer and more independent than at any
time in its previous history. Taneyef retained
his counterpoint class, but the principal piano
students were transferred to the care of Safonof,
whom Taneyef had invited from Petrograd at the
beginning of his rule, and who now became
Director. Taneyef remained on the staff until

1906, when, owing to a disagreement with Safonof in regard to the conduct of the Conservatoire, he retired, causing, as Lyadof expressed it in a published letter, a very heavy loss to that institution.

(3)

Taneyef composed very slowly, and his last example is numbered Opus 36. But despite his busy life he found time to include in that number a variety of important works. One of his earliest compositions was the Cantata, *St. John of Damascus*, to the text of Alexis Tolstoi, and dedicated to the memory of Nicholas Rubinstein; this was produced in 1892 at Moscow. In later life he wrote a further work in this form, based on Khomiakof's *On Reading a Psalm*, in which he far out-distanced the earlier example. This was not performed until after his death, when it was hailed as a work of great dignity. He published but one of his three symphonies, that written in 1898 and dedicated to Glazounof, and one opera, or, as he preferred to call it, Operatic Trilogy, based on the *Orestes* of Æschylus. This was mounted at the Maryinsky Theatre, Petrograd, in October, 1895, and withdrawn very soon after on account of the composer's quite justifiable objection to a number of "cuts" made in the performance. It was revived shortly after his death. Taneyef wrote a number of vocal works both for solo and chorus, but it is in the sphere of chamber-music that his best work was done, and in his six string quartets and other instrumental music of this class he has left a series of splendid contributions to a literature hitherto somewhat neglected by his compatriots. One of his earliest compositions was a chorus on Pushkin's *Exegi Monumentum*, performed on the unveiling of a memorial to that poet in Moscow in 1880. A few years later he began that colossal work, the *Manual of Counterpoint*, which occupied him for twenty years, and which seems likely to prove a durable monument to Taneyef's activities, both as a composer and as a teacher. Shortly before his death he expressed the intention of issuing an abridged edition. There exists, however, a still more notable and possibly less perishable testimony to his qualities as a teacher. The list of his famous pupils, headed by the names of Skryabin and Rakhmaninof, is as long as that associated with his friend Rimsky-Korsakof, and bears witness as eloquently to his capacity for endowing those who worked under him with a thorough musicianship.

Taneyef died of a heart affection on June 6th, 1915, at Dioutkof, in the Government of Zveni-gorod, whither he had repaired as usual for the holidays, and was buried at the Donsky Monastery,

his funeral attracting a large number of musicians
eager to pay a last tribute to the dead composer.
An extensive library of valuable books and manuscripts was bequeathed to the Moscow Music
Library, which he had himself been instrumental
in founding.

(4)

So exacting an artist was Taneyef, says a Russian
writer, that he would not allow to be printed a
single bar that gave him less than full satisfaction.
To his thoroughness, a characteristic revealing
itself in every direction in which one may seek
for a revelation of the composer's personality, is
to be assigned the cause of the smallness of his
published output. Thus, although Taneyef is
known to have completed three symphonies—the
first (in E minor) a scholastic exercise begun in
1873, the second in D minor, dedicated to Arensky,
written in 1884 and performed a year later by the
Imperial Russian Musical Society, and the third
(in C minor), Opus 12, a work often played in
Russia—only the last-named has been published.
From more than one source we have information
as to the laboriousness of Taneyef's creative process. In Rimsky-Korsakof's Memoirs the author
tells of an extreme " niceness " in the selection of
thematic material, and of the many experiments

made with it before its inclusion was finally decided upon. Glazounof compares this procedure with that of Schubert, who, when composing in the larger forms, rehearsed a series of adventures for his themes, adopting them only after a searching scrutiny of the transmutations they had undergone.

The C minor symphony, dedicated to Glazounof, which is in the usual four movements— Allegro molto, Adagio, Scherzo and Allegro energico—is not a work which will ever attract vast multitudes to the concert-hall as have been drawn there by the symphonies of Taneyef's teacher. Neither by his themes nor by his orchestral resources does he make anything like a popular appeal. The music of this work has been described as possessing an " eternal " quality, but its permanent value lies in its perfection of formal beauty rather than in thematic allurements or cumulative instrumental effect. In the later years of his life he became more inclined to sanction the presence of a reserved kind of romanticism in music ; this may be attributed to his contact with the Petrograd musicians and the influence of some of his progressive pupils ; but the C minor symphony, written in 1898, reflects, as strongly as any instrumental work from Taneyef's pen, his reverence for the classic masters. In the Adagio, however, he reveals a depth of feeling which, if it does not recall the mood of the beautiful Largo of the quartet, Opus 4, provides at least some moments in which the composer allows himself to assure us that his heart as well as his head has influenced its writing.

In the matter of instrumentation, even in the symphony Taneyef reveals that he is not averse from enlarging the classical orchestra, but he is evidently not prepared to avail himself of any of the picturesque effects that enter into the scheme of most writers for the orchestra, even those who also have a great respect for the past. Taneyef employs here a contrabassoon, four horns, three trumpets and three trombones, but nothing in the category of " percussion " beyond *timpani*. Such devices as are absent from this score are as a rule found only in music that has another purpose than a search for sheer beauty of sound and conciseness of form.

(5)

It is in an earlier work, that numbered Opus 1, that Taneyef indulges in some degree in music of a more personal, if not precisely of a subjective, kind. The Cantata, *St. John of Damascus*, for chorus and orchestra, dating from 1884, was begun soon after the death of Nicholas Rubinstein, which had occurred in Paris in 1881. This work, which is written to a text of Alexis Tolstoi, while utterly different in every way from Tchaikovsky's tribute to his former colleague—the celebrated Trio—is said to contain moments in which the measure of Taneyef's sense of loss is revealed, and, in places where the text allows of the betrayal of a personal expression of grief, Taneyef has written music which is particularly impressive.

This description may well be applied to the instrumental introduction, the theme of which is referred to in the middle of the work, being employed in augmentation at its conclusion as the subject of a choral fugue. In contrast to Tchaikovsky's lament, Taneyef's Cantata contains its message of consolation, and the mood of an Andante sostenuto in D flat is that of hope. *St. John of Damascus* was performed under its composer's conductorship in 1892, at Moscow, and was revived in 1910 for the jubilee celebration of the founding, by Nicholas Rubinstein, of the local branch of the Imperial Russian Musical Society.

In a work in similar form the composer has left a product of his matured creative powers. This is the Cantata for soloists, chorus and orchestra, written to the words of Khomiakof's *On Reading a Psalm*. It consists of three independent sections. An introductory chorus, an Aria, leading to the final chorus, and a fugue with three subjects have been singled out as particularly fine numbers, and, in the latter, it is declared, the composer excelled himself. In the opinion of one writer, however, the work is too impersonal, and a comparison is made between Taneyef's writing and the impression left by similar examples of Mendelssohn's music, such as *Elijah* and *St. Paul*, in which, despite the composer's almost fanatical reverence for Bach, his individuality is shown on every page. We are reminded on referring to another critic that the personal point of view must be taken into consideration, for, in this case, Taneyef receives a congratulation on having effaced himself, on having written in a strain of reserved and noble lyricism, the source of which is traced to Tchaikovsky, without falling into the subjective method of expression justly associated with the latter. The last-quoted critic refers to Taneyef's contrapuntal developments which, far from being a mere dry " working-out," proclaim the composer to be without an equal in this domain, and avers that while its mastery cannot be appreciated at a first hearing, the effect of the Cantata's emotional content is immediate. The fact that Taneyef has so successfully adopted a secular form for material of a devotional order is spoken of as being immensely significant to Russian musicians.

(6)

Were the fact not already known to him, no one would be more surprised than the attentive student of Taneyef's orchestral, choral and chamber-music, to learn that this composer had written an opera. The incredulity of such an individual would surely be increased when he heard that *Orestes*, Taneyef's only work in dramatic form, shows clear traces of Wagnerian influence. This curious sport from Taneyef's creative growth may be coupled with his early *Overture on Russian Themes*, composed during a period in which he was giving a great deal of consideration to the question of musical nationalism. What seems far more in keeping with the composer's character is that he approached the operatic enterprise in the manner of one about to undertake the compilation of a treatise on the subject rather than to pour out the fruits of a profound dramatic and musical inspiration. As is proved by the recently published Correspondence, the query answered by Tchaikovsky, who, in 1891, gave his opinion that opera writing should be regarded as a product of a divine gift rather than of human contrivance, was not the first mention of Taneyef's project. Already, in July, 1887, he confided to his master and friend the secret that he had begun the work. A year later he was writing about the draft of the third act. He was a "greatly interested" listener on the occasion of Neumann's Wagner Festival in April, 1889, and reported in July that his opera was progressing, "though slowly." But, when asking Tchaikovsky's advice, Taneyef had apparently in mind a second edition of the libretto, for though he had finished the first act, which had occupied him for no less than seven years, he spoke of a number of radical changes of plan, observing that the slowness of composition was really quite advantageous in his case, as he had discarded many ideas which, he could only rejoice, had not been allowed to remain in the opera. In this letter (January 14th, 1891), in the writing of which he spent five hours, he gives an illuminating account of his creative process. " The second benefit derived from my slowness is that it has allowed me to apply to the composition of my opera a system which, so far as I am concerned, and according to my conviction, is the very best method." This, to judge by his explanation, appears to be a modification of the Spencerian or "synthetic" plan; he styles it a "concentric method." Opera, he says, should not be composed by stringing together a number of independently conceived and successively written items, but "in proceeding from whole to details : from opera to acts, from acts to scenes, from scenes to separate numbers. Working under these conditions the crucial points of the opera can be observed at an early stage, on them the composer's attention is advantageously concentrated—he can easily determine the length of scenes and numbers, the modulatory plan of the acts . . ." Further passages in this " amazingly lengthy " letter assure us that Rimsky-Korsakof's account of Taneyef's method of composition contains no exaggeration, and, further, that the system that sounds so simple does not exhaust the scientific labour of operatic creation. " On my themes . . . I write contrapuntal exercises, canons, imitations, etc. In the course of time, from all this chaos of separate ideas and snippets, emerges something more orderly and definite . . ." After perusing such passages as these we are quite ready to join the composer of *Sadko* in marvelling that *Orestes* contains nevertheless some moments of real beauty.

Orestes in its final form consists of three small operas : the first, " Agamemnon," contains two tableaux which occupy only twenty and forty-one minutes, respectively, in performance. The second part is called " Choephori," and the third " Eumenides," thus conforming to the plan of the " Father of Tragedy." The libretto by Benkstern is, as one would expect, on a level of merit in keeping with Taneyef's ideals.

Cheshikin, who deals with the work at some

length, avers that the greatest fault in *Orestes* is a total absence of archaic colouring. The author of *The Russian Opera* admits that there are few surviving indications of what such colouring ought to be, but considers that a judicious employment of the ancient modes would not have been amiss. Taneyef, emulating Serof, has adopted the Wagnerian method, and the leading motive principle is exploited, and " if he does not achieve Wagnerian effects he has written many beautiful pages . . ." The *entr'acte* to the second tableau of " Eumenides," described as being vividly descriptive, Clytemnestra's lyrical Arioso with chorus in " Agamemnon," and the scene of Orestes with the Eumenides, " recalling Gluck's furies," are singled out for special mention.

Orestes received its first performance on October 17th, 1895. The public seem to have taken kindly to it ; but the " cuts," which are alleged by Rimsky-Korsakof to have been made by Napravnik, were not to the composer's liking, and, as in the absence of an agreement he had no legal remedy, he elected to withdraw the work. There were compensations ; discussion of his grievance among the Petrograd musical circle reached the ears of Belayef, who came forward with a proposal to publish *Orestes*, hitherto existing only in a lithographed edition, and it was issued by his firm in 1900. After the composer's death the work was revived, and given on the scene of its original produ&ion.

(7)

The name of Belayef will long be honoured as having been borne by one through whose efforts Russian chamber-music has been endowed with a significance almost equal—with due regard to the proportionate popularity of the two arts—to that of opera. The realists of the 'sixties were pre-occupied with those forms of music which could interpret life : with Song, and especially with Music-Drama. But with the turn of the tide—the idealism of the 'eighties synchronizing with a return to the pure instrumental forms— chamber-music naturally began to claim the attention of composers. Of the nationalist group Borodin is alone to be credited with a masterpiece, and, but for his experience as a player, would probably never have thought of entering this arena.

When, following upon the debut of Glazounof, Belayef took a central position in Petrograd musical society, he, also able to participate in performances of chamber-music, began to encourage the composers grouped around him to express their thoughts in this more intimate language. His historic " Fridays " were instituted, and Russian chamber-music began to earn its title to consideration as an art-manifestation having certain distinctive characteristics. Many of the works produced by the Petrograd group possess qualities which contribute to the significance of this denomination. The *Novelettes* of Glazounof, the dedicatory works inspired by Belayef's idealistic regard for music, the collaborative series in which several composers united in creating a well-proportioned collection out of a number of exquisite miniatures, have resulted in creating a new impression, not merely of chamber-music in Russia but of Russian music in other countries. Had the Russians elected to follow the path trodden in the posthumous quartets of Beethoven, we should at this moment perhaps still be labouring under the false impression that Russian music was nothing but a reflection of gloom, an engraving of a musical picture whose subject was similar either to that in which Moussorgsky painted the anguish of Boris or to Tchaikovsky's vivid symphonic descriptions of his own. These *Variations on a popular Russian theme*, and these " Friday " collections, tell a very different tale, one which provokes merriment in regard to their content and admiration in respect of their wonderful mastery.

(8)

The chamber-music left by Taneyef has very little in common with the product of the Petrograd optimists. The Moscow composer, despite his indebtedness to Belayef, acknowledged in the dedication of the string quartet, Opus 16, and his esteem for Rimsky-Korsakof, expressed by means of the employment of themes from *Sadko* in the fugal variation in his first work in this form, did not join, as did Skryabin, in the collaborative works with which the tradition of the joint *Mlada* opera-ballet and the " Chop-sticks " piano variations was perpetuated. The part he played in Russian chamber-music was that of providing a number of works which should testify to a native capacity for writing in the traditional or classical style ; it is part of an achievement in which he shares with Glazounof and Rimsky-Korsakof the distinction of having proved to the world, on behalf of Russian musicians as a body, that they were not all soldiers, sailors and chemists with a taste for composition ! The importance of Taneyef's contribution to Russian chamber-music lies in its power of maintaining that while the Petrograd composers have given us new forms, and have returned to a mood of gaiety that since Haydn had been gradually superseded by one of austerity, there is, or was, one in Moscow who, for sheer dexterity in part-writing and for scholarliness as a whole, is unsurpassed by any modern creative musician in the world.

Taneyef's chamber-music is distinguished by

its quality as well as by its relative quantity. Numbering in all thirteen works (there is also one unpublished piano trio, dating from the late 'seventies), comprising six quartets, two string quintets, two string trios, a piano quintet, quartet and trio, his product fully contributes to the consolidation of the literature of Russian chamber-music. But its quality is to be regarded, from the point of view of expressiveness, as relatively a defect. Perfection of form, mastery of construction, both as to the whole and the details, cannot atone for an absence of poetical ideas, an absence the more conspicuous since the composer has clearly aimed at expressing himself poetically, especially, as need hardly be mentioned, in his slow movements. Taneyef's themes are recognizable by students of his works as symbols of expressiveness ; they are the equivalent of the beautiful melodies which have flowed spontaneously from the heart, through the pen, of many an inspired composer ; perhaps one may say that they serve their turn in providing a relief from the pattern-weaving, so absorbing to the attention of the intelligent listener. To apply a crude measure to the poetic merits of Taneyef's chamber-music and to inquire which of his movements has been, or ever will be, isolated from its context and given a detached performance, seems perhaps like inviting the payment of what is usually, in such cases,

a rather doubtful compliment, and even a dis-
service, to sheer loveliness. But by this rough and
ready method it is possible to establish a comparison, to institute a proper differentiation between Taneyef's chamber-music and that of
almost every other composer of distinction, even
of Brahms, whom, by the way, he much disliked.

(9)

Yet although Taneyef is to be reckoned among
the more classical-minded writers for the quartet
and other of the chamber combinations, although
we must reckon that once removed from the
romanticist influence—betrayed both in the dedication of his first string quartet (Opus 4, to
Tchaikovsky) and by ¦its content—he wrote in a
manner both idealistic and objective, although
we feel assured by such passages as the opening of
the Finale of the second string quartet (Opus 5),
by the tremendously ingenious Allegro molto of
the fifth (Opus 13), and by the occasional appearance of fugal movements and the many exhibitions
of a delight in wielding a supreme contrapuntal
mastery, this composer has not been satisfied
merely to erect an edifice destined to house tablets
to the memory of past masters.

In Opus 5 he begins by reviving the grave
humour of Bach and the jocosity of Haydn ; in

the eighth variation of Opus 7 there is a jolliness quite Haydnesque, followed by an unexpected return, in the last page, to the principal subject of the first part, resembling the Beethovenian type of " surprise " ; but the Mazurka variation in the same work already prepares us to expect that this mood will be reflected sooner or later in something equally diverting, but couched in more modern a vein, and this anticipation is realized in the bold figuration of the Vivace con fuoco of the string quintet (Opus 14). This is rather the high-spirited humour of a man of our day than the infectious gaiety of a Haydn, or the sparkling prattle of a Mozart, as one might characterize the mood and manner of the *Giga* of the sixth quartet (Opus 19).

Again, this master of form was not content to abide by the stereotyped pattern of the four-movement plan, as is shown, for instance, in the arrangement of the quartet (Opus 13) in A, where, after an Adagio which succeeds the opening Allegro, he adopts the unusual course of writing two successive quick movements, having already in his first chamber-work broken away from the conventional number. In the string Trio (Opus 21), he publishes his allegiance to the masters with whom the Menuetto was a customary movement, reproducing also their style ; it is in the variations that he shows best how an observance of the past may be coupled with a regard for the future vitality of music. Testimony to a desire to establish Russian music on a firm footing is provided by his employment of every known instrumental chamber-combination—short of those in which wind enters—and having emulated Dvorak with a Trio for two violins and viola he avails himself of a newly-fashioned instrument, the tenor-viola, as the third voice in the second string Trio. The compass of the tenor-viola lies between that of the alto and 'cello; the instrument is constructed by Vitaček, of Moscow, on the lines of one built in 1848 at Warzburg, and recently presented to the museum of Moscow Conservatoire by Professor von Glehn, who designed the modern example for which Taneyef has written.

That Taneyef's style, particularly that of his melodies, belongs to a remote generation, is not surprising in view of his profound knowledge and, at times, almost meticulous study of the standard works of Bach and his immediate successors. But, as already stated, other influences are betrayed. Passages in the Allegro of the second quintet and the first movement of the quintet (Opus 16) recall the rhythmic mannerisms of Brahms, the general colour of his first work for stringed instruments adds much point to the dedication to Tchaikovsky; while the occasional *cadenza*—the one in the quintet inscribed to Rimsky-Korsakof is quite an elaborate affair—shows that the composer of *Sheherazade* was not alone in desiring to confer upon individual instruments the rights of citizenship he sought on their behalf.

But in indicating such influenced characteristics in Taneyef's chamber-music, it behoves one to point out that he was chiefly influenced by his own lofty idealism. He did not care sufficiently for the piano to give the usual undue prominence to that instrument in the works wherein it figures, and the impression left by them is that he is striving to approach, as near as may be, to faultlessness of design, leaving material that commands respect or even reverence, but has no great power of arousing emotion.

(10)

As a writer for the voice, apart from works on the grand scale in which a chorus is associated with an orchestra, Taneyef composed several concerted examples among which are two quartets *a capella*, *The Monastery on Kasbek* and *Adela*. So many Russians have been inspired by the Caucasus that one is not astonished to find, among Taneyef's letters, an enthusiastic description of that wonderful territory ; that he was not capable of vividly reproducing those impressions in music is borne out partly by the first-mentioned

number, and also by the absence of any other
attempt to reproduce them. His other concerted
vocal works, for which class he had a particular
affection, include three lyric choruses *a capella*,
a five and a six-part chorus on Balmont's texts,
and two others, in seven and eight groups, to
words of Polonsky, a poet whose choice of musical
subjects brought him under the notice of other
composers.

Taneyef wrote in all about forty songs, but this
fruitfulness is not betrayed in the numbering of
his works, since they are published in groups, that
marked Opus 17 accounting for no less than ten.
Here he covers a fairly wide field of poetry, setting
texts of Shelley (in the Balmont re-creations),
Fet, Nekrassof, A. Tolstoi and others. These
are remarkable principally for their absolute simplicity. One imagines the composer making a
determined effort to avoid all harmonic or contrapuntal complexity. One would hardly expect a
composer who had chosen such lines, for instance,
as Shelley's *The Isle*, to deny himself the musician's
prerogative of free description ; yet Taneyef, as
though fearing that his musical version might lead
the listener even further away from the original
than that of Balmont, is content to write music
which comes as near the " absolute " as could well
be. Only in the Nocturne of this set do the words
(of Shcherbin) evoke music that, by comparison

with the rest, can be called florid, leaving an impression of romanticism which may be traceable, to judge by the character of its melodic line, to the influence of Wagner.

In the later songs one finds the same occasional outburst of feeling, but no great advance in harmonic colouring, and in the first of the Polonsky set (1910), *In Time of Loss*, as in the final number, *A Winter Journey*, the music is characterized by the extreme simplicity of the early works of this kind, only the former having any descriptive material—if one may safely so term the two bars following the mention of " tears that flow as from a spring." One notable feature of the general freedom from extravagance in Taneyef's songs is the evenness and vocalistic quality of the melodic line ; this at least may induce singers to bring forward some examples which, in default of any striking emotional or tuneful qualities, have at any rate that of artistic purity in a degree rare enough in vocal literature.

MEDTNER

CHAPTER VIII

MEDTNER

(1)

It is easily to be seen that Russia, at present the most progressive country in musical affairs, is not at all lacking in the conservative spirit. From the beginning of the movement initiated with the purpose of endowing music with a deeper significance and of establishing a closer relationship between music and life—a movement which will probably recur as long as the art exists, though it may not each time be called Romanticism—there has been an opposing body which has manifested a concern deeper in regard to form than to content. The history of Russia's musical emancipation, if carefully studied and with due detachment—a rather difficult matter in view of the strong bias discoverable in the volumes of Russian historians —will reveal that, without this conserving and consolidating force, Russian music might have been looked upon by the outside world as an experimental effort, as a phenomenon that could perhaps be given a presentable artistic shape if taken over by experienced artists and subjected to a polishing and finishing process. The world of Russian music would have presented itself as being peopled with composers who, like Goussakovsky and Ladijensky, both early adherents of the Balakiref group, improvised a great deal but actually wrote exceedingly little, with progressive artists like Moussorgsky, whose practical technical knowledge was insufficient, or like Borodin, whose capacity for musical thought was greater than his appetite for musical action.

Rimsky-Korsakof, as we know, foresaw the danger and forearmed himself, subsequently fighting and winning a great battle on behalf of Russian nationalist music. During the period of our first experiences of Russian opera, one of the London musical critics recorded a remark overheard when leaving the theatre after a performance of Borodin's *Prince Igor*, an opera left unfinished by the composer to be completed by other hands. The observation, uttered by a rather inexperienced and decidedly puzzled student of the subject, was to the effect that Russian opera always seemed to have been " written by someone else." So far as concerns nationalist opera, that " someone else " was usually Rimsky-Korsakof. But times have changed, and although the outlook upon music, in the case of such a composer as Skryabin, is far removed from anything discernible in previous musical history, there must be few who would be so bold as to declare that anyone else could have better expressed Skryabin's thoughts in music than that composer himself. If Skryabin's art is considered experimental in nature there is no gainsaying the mastery with which the experiment has been conducted.

In the Petrograd School we see, at the present time, the conservative work of Rimsky-Korsakof being carried on, with a greater insistence on matters of form, by Glazounof—the principal, at this moment, of the Conservatoire. In Moscow there has always been a deep respect for the architectonic element in music, and Taneyef was, perhaps, the greatest enthusiast in the world for the enlargement of the polyphonic function, in the increased activity of which he saw the vitality of music in the future. But the romantic spirit did not enter deeply into Taneyef's musical nature. In the art of his pupil Rakhmaninof romanticism is all-pervading, and perfection of structure appears to have been only a secondary' consideration.

(2)

There is a composer who is to be placed midway between the two, an artist in much of whose music is to be discerned evidences of deep personal feeling, but whose reverence for formal purity is unexampled in any living creative artist, and that is Medtner. The spirit of his music is that of the great romanticists of the past, strengthened by experience of the modern world. Thus, while he is more romantic than his precursors, he is, in comparison with other moderns such as Skryabin, Stravinsky and the younger men, positively a classicist. When his music contains the element of the unexpected, it is the wealth of harmony which surprises, and not its " unusualness." Medtner is in the direct " constitutional " line of music, considered as an expressive art, and it is thought that he may prove a Titan, even in comparison with his mighty precursors.

Of that it is not yet possible to be confident, because, with all the obvious signs of mental activity and poetic sensibility, we have to judge their product as expressed upon a comparatively restricted instrument. Up to the present Medtner has written a large number of piano pieces, abundant songs, a sonata for piano and violin, and three nocturnes for the same instrumental pair. A creative artist who might well have chosen the symphonic poem as the most appropriate medium in which to express himself, has confined himself to the " domestic " musical forms, and by his output in such forms we must for the present judge him.

Nicholas Medtner was born on December 24th, 1879, in Moscow. His parents were German ;

but one gleans from his first vocal text, derived from Lermontof, that their educational scheme did not entirely exclude the poets of their adoptive country. There is no record of those precocious efforts in composition or performance usually associated with genius in embryo, and the first published work—a song to the words of Lermontof's " Angel "—was not issued until 1896, or five years after Medtner had entered the Moscow Conservatoire. This, together with the first number of the *Three Improvisations* (Opus 2), which belong to the same year, must be looked upon to some extent as the fruit of study. At the Conservatoire he had the good fortune to fall into the hands of Safonof, whose splendid training has given to Russia some fine composer-pianists, among them Rakhmaninof and Skryabin, both of whom, like Medtner, developed an exceptional interpretative faculty. In 1900 Medtner was awarded the gold medal, and, leaving the Conservatoire, proceeded to enter the " Rubinstein " competition for piano-playing, which brought him a further trophy. After such a triumphant beginning the young man found no difficulty in obtaining engagements, and for the next two years he was occupied in displaying his pianistic gifts before Russian and German audiences. Subsequently he returned to his *alma mater* as professor of his instrument, a position he has continued to hold, with a lapse of one year, devoted exclusively to composition. His recitals and his appearances in chamber-concerts are always eagerly anticipated by Moscow audiences.

(3)

In his creative work Medtner evinced, at the outset, a curious restlessness in regard to style, title and form. As to the latter, it may be mentioned that the Lermontof song already spoken of, and the first number of the *Acht Stimmungsbilder* for piano, which bears a quotation from the former's text, consist of identical musical material, are both numbered Opus 1, and that no explanation is offered for this repetition. The German titular heading of the amplified Opus 1 is replaced in Opus 2 by a French title, *Trois Improvisations*, to the separate numbers of which there are German sub-titles. In Opus 4, *Quatre Morceaux*, the sub-titles are French. The F minor sonata, the publication of which the composer entrusted to Belayef, bears the ambi-lingual announcement customary with that firm, but from that time until his abandonment of his first publisher, Jurgenson, and his entry into a contract with the Russian Music Publishing Company, Medtner's compositions were given a German primary description—with two curious exceptions—the settings of

Heine and Goethe, Opp. 12 and 15, which, despite their literary material, are described in Russian. In the music itself one notices a gradual progress towards a Russian manner, particularly in the vocal line of his songs. Already in Opus 13 (composed in 1903), for the two texts of which Medtner drew upon such widely different poets as Pushkin and André Biely, we find in No. 1, " Winter Evening," an interlude which serves for the introduction of a song quite in the folk-manner ; in Opus 24, the melody to which Tioutchef's lines are set (in the second of the series), is again Russian in flavour ; the same poet's words, in Opus 28, " Spring's Tranquillity," are given a modal setting ; while in the Pushkin set, Opus 29 (published in 1914), there is ample evidence, both in No. 2, " The Singer "—which is faintly reminiscent of the introduction to Lel's third song in *The Snowmaiden*—in No. 4, " Why dost thou neigh, my fiery steed," and in the last number, " Exorcism," of a desire to render a service to the country of the composer's birth.

But ere reaching the Slavonic mode of expression observable in such recent examples as the three pieces, Opus 31—particularly in the first—Medtner has passed through an Odyssey of influences, the most conspicuous of which is that of Brahms, with whom he made a sojourn in what may for the moment be reckoned as the middle period. If in the earliest work the indications of that which later became a marked tendency were somewhat faint until the first sonata, Opus 5 in F minor, the influence showed itself a good deal more clearly at certain moments, both as to rhythmic pattern and harmony, in the Goethe songs, Opus 15, in " She loves me " from *Erwin and Elmire*, and perhaps a little less in *From Lila* and " My love is near." But it is in the incomparable *Three Nocturnes* for piano and violin, Opus 16, and the sonata for these instruments, that the search for rhythmic diversity is most noticeable, and their harmonic colouring suggests, at the same time, that there has been a close study of the German master. Interesting evidences of his approach to the Brahmsian manner are to be found in the first of the *Sonaten-Triade*, Opus 11, in which the rhythmic pattern becomes more complex than heretofore, and of his departure therefrom in the *Sonata-Skazka*, Opus 25, No. 1 ; in the beautiful dignity of the second movement of this—an Andante con moto—one feels that the Chopinistic lyrical vein, which reveals itself in an early stage of the composer's development, is again coming to the surface, but is purified of its more indulgent qualities by contact with an element of austerity.

MEDTNER.

(4)

In the array of attributes which go to form the
individuality of a composer, unless he has lived
altogether aloof from the world of music and
remote from the influences that a hearing of
masterpieces is bound to exert upon even the most
independent creative mind, there must be found
certain features which recall those of the great
musical prophets whose music has constituted the
main pabulum of his education. In some cases,
as in that of Skryabin—and certain instances are
to be discovered nearer home—the young artist
becomes pre-occupied with the style and substance of one particular composer, a pre-occupa-
tion that borders at times upon idolization. In
Medtner, who so often forcibly reminds one of
Brahms, one can hardly fail to recognize, in the
early works, the presence of a quality somewhat
tenderer, more lyrical and genial. But the tender-
ness of the *Eight Mood-Pictures*, Opus I, does not
ever become over-compassionate, or sentimental,
the lyricism is not allowed to proceed to the extreme of mere tunefulness, the geniality stops far
short of expansiveness. And with Medtner, the
word " influence " must not be supposed to imply,
as often it is, either plagiarism or downright
imitation. There is the same difference between
its application in his case and in that of many other

composers, as exists between the use of the word " programme " in relation to Beethoven's *Eroica* symphony and its employment again, without qualification, to describe the " Pastoral." In Medtner's music one discerns what may be an inherent or a cultivated sympathy with Chopin, Schumann, at one or two odd moments with Grieg, and at others with neo-Debussism, but with a few exceptions—as for instance the florid Chopinistic *Quasi-Valse* (the last number of Opus 1) and the *Maestoso Freddo* (No. 3), which recalls the same master in a chastened mood, the second of the *Drei Märchen*, Opus 9, and the third *Lyric Fragment*, Opus 23—"influence" has itself been influenced by the composer's own individuality ; and in this there is a strain of austerity and reserve which brings him nearer to the German composer with whom he has so often been compared than to any other master in the history of music; Medtner is, in fact, a modern Brahms. He is, perhaps, rather more exuberant, but such exuberance is that of an abstract musical and not a pictorial conception ; he may reach greater emotional heights, but the emotion never suggests a profoundly personal origin, it belongs to the composer's musical and not his personal self. On the whole he is better represented by the smooth course pursued in the music of the sonata (Opus 22) than by the more passionate and heroically emotional substance of the later example in E minor, Opus 25, No. 2 (dedicated to Rakhmaninof); but while marking these out as typical, the third of the *Four Tales*, Opus 26, must be mentioned as characteristic of Medtner in the dreamier mood. This little piece is very like Chopin, although the transitional passage, *cantando*, could never have been written by the Pole ; but putting this aside, the whole musical fabric is tempered by its passage through Medtner's mind ; he expresses a sentiment which is eternal, but his manner of expressing it belongs to an age in which the artist is inclined to reserve his attention for essentials, and to discard everything with which he can safely dispense.

As a further contrast to this poetic mood, we have in the Finale of the magnificent violin sonata, and the last movement of the sonata, Opus 5, an heroic—and in the last instance almost a titanic—manner. In these examples the composer seems to be revelling in a technique that enables him to pile up tremendous climaxes, dictated by an emotion engendered by his contemplation of the music's progress, without being hampered by an undue concern about technical matters. Medtner combines the skill of the supreme craftsman with the poetic feeling of the inspired musician, and the sincerity of the true artist.

(5)

It is not only in the manipulation of an orthodox harmonic scheme and a display of a complete mastery over the contrapuntal method that Medtner takes the art of music a step further along the broad road travelled by his great forerunners. He is apparently aware that a living art needs an occasional change of mould in order that free expansion may be secured for it. And as the artist is naturally concerned with the accommodation, in a form suited to them, of his own musical conceptions, Medtner has invented musical art-forms that are designed for his own use and are quite likely to fail in suiting other composers. He has found a musical equivalent of his own emotions, the fruit of his experience of life, and being an artist of strong feeling he is not satisfied to arrange them in the shapes which have already served to enclose the expressions of earlier musicians.

To this search for a suitable mould we doubtless owe the novel generic titles borne by his compositions. These "Lyric Fragments," "Improvisations," "Tragedy-Fragments," "Fables," "Dithyrambs," "Novels," "Sonata-Triads," "Sonata-Tales," and "Sonata-Ballads" are not likely to become conventionalized forms; they are not destined to serve like that more liberal designation, the Symphonic Poem, to clothe the ideas of a variety of creative artists having divergent aims. They are part and parcel of Medtner's musical scheme, and belong perhaps solely to him. Moreover, the music to which they are affixed does not illustrate these designations in the highly coloured fashion or with that obviousness that might attract the smaller-minded, the merely talented composer. In the *Lyric Fragments*, for instance, there is no sudden burst of song ; the lyricism, as well as the piece, is fragmentary. The *Improvisations* are perhaps better described by their titles, for the primary thought is kept pretty well to the fore throughout the piece in each case. The two *Tragedy-Fragments* do not contain anything of an intensely dramatic nature, nor are the *Fables* particularly suggestive. Of the *Novels*, the second and third do perhaps contain the musical equivalent of a plot, but the initial piece has a serenely pastoral quality. The slow movement of the *Sonata-Tale* may faintly suggest a narratory manner, and the recurrence of its theme during the course of the subsequent Allegro con Spirito apparently sanctions the assumption that there is a literary basis to this music.

Had Medtner dedicated such works as his *Novels* and *Tales* to novelists and story-tellers, one would have less readily stated the belief that his titles are born of the union of a transient intellectual condition with a somewhat more permanent musical mood.

These titular designations, conceived by a musical aristocrat and not likely to be vulgarized by imitators, are not, then, to be regarded as making Medtner any less of an " abstract " musician. The sentiment of the pieces they adorn—and the titles are clearly more ornamental than essential—though possibly making an effect on the subconscious, reveals no definite image to the conscious mind. In the first of the two *Fables*, Opus 14, the programmatic element seems strangely neglected ; there is, as it were, no central figure in a canvas that seems to demand one.

Medtner's piano music could hardly be described as fulfilling the destiny required of all music by Moussorgsky : that of facilitating human intercourse. It is music better enjoyed in the playing than in the hearing.

(6)

Medtner is one of the most distinguished representatives of that modern Russian school in which craftsmanship has been developed in a high degree with the conscious purpose of causing facility to become second nature. But having gained his freedom, having contrived to endow his musical

limbs with an unexampled flexibility, it is
only natural that he should have availed himself somewhat to excess of the facility obtained.
This becomes noticeable as he attains what has
been called the middle period, and it is in the
violin sonata, Opus 21, that we find a jostling of
ideas which cannot all be simultaneously assimilated by anyone but the person to whom the
privilege of interpretation has fallen. A certain
callousness towards the mere listener is already
observable in the writing of the sonata, Opus 5 ;
in its last movement are passages which fit
admirably into the scheme, and are gratifying
when offered on the printed page to the eye, but,
rendered on the piano, the excessively low chro-
matic scale-figures produce a tonal muddiness ;
the fault may be characterized in this instance as
the equivalent of inferior instrumentation. At
the time of its composition, Medtner seems to
have been a rather unsocial composer, who wrote
for himself and his kind ; presently he began to
realize his error, to apologize for his want of consideration, and to furnish secondary and simpler
versions of the most difficult passages, with an
occasional aid to their execution. There are, of
course, among the latest works, examples in which
simplicity cannot be said to prevail ; the decidedly
complex Improvisation, Opus 31, is in reality,
however, a series of variations, a form in which

Medtner could hardly be expected to write simply.

(7)

In the songs there is a greater restraint until the Tioutchef set, Opus 24, when the voice receives less consideration and is frequently in danger of being effaced by the exuberant accompaniment. But in this respect most of his subsequent vocal examples follow the method pursued in the enchanting Nocturnes for piano and violin rather than that of the sonata, and in the last numbers of the seven Pushkin poems he is content with a relative simplicity, both harmonic and rhythmic.

It is in the songs that one notices most often Medtner's extraordinary fertility of idea. His resource is such that every song seems to have an entirely fresh scheme. Reading through a large number of examples by one composer, one expects to discover, and is prepared to condone, an occasional reminiscence. With Medtner there is hardly ever a hint of a previous idea, each poem or text seems to have inspired a completely fresh musical conception. One may make so bold as to suggest, if not to assert, that a series of recitals devoted to Medtner's sixty odd vocal pieces would prove as rich a feast as could be provided by a number of composers chosen from the foremost representatives of the musical family to which he belongs. And he achieves this amazing variety without calling in the quite legitimate aid of musical description. Here and there one finds examples in which there is something more than the reflection of a mood ; in the setting of Nietzsche's " Despair," Opus 19, No. 2, the presence of a bell figure proves to us that Medtner does not altogether look askance at devices of this kind, and while we look in vain for suggestions of the pastoral in the Heine song, " Hill Voices," Opus 12, No. 3, we shall find in the first number of the above-cited set that the song of the lark—an episode in Nietzsche's " Home-coming "—is given in the music with a definiteness that is apt to surprise one when it is remembered that the music is Medtner's, and one more example approaching closer to pure imitation is the echo of Damon's flute in " The Convert," after Goethe.

It might perhaps be gathered from the estimate here made of his songs, from the tribute paid to his unfailing rhythmic resourcefulness and his avoidance of the stereotyped, both in harmonic texture and melodic line, that Medtner is a composer whose music is devoid of mannerism. One can hardly thus brand his generous employment of so universal a rhythmic expedient as syncopation nor could one wish to deprive any composer who evinces a fondness for rhythmic pattern-weaving of so helpful a device. But those who devote themselves to an attentive perusal of Medtner's music will not be long in discovering a few instances of figuration which recurs with sufficient frequency to become noticeable. Of such may be mentioned the demi-semiquaver group repeated several times in one of the *Erwin and Elmire* songs of Opus 6, which is seen again in the second set of Goethe songs (Opus 15) and once more in the noble violin Nocturne in C. This, together with an occasional repetition of a melodic turn and the recurrence of a harmonic idea, such as may be identified by comparing the first *Novel* with the *Danza* movement of the violin sonata, appears to exhaust everything in the nature of *cliché* with which Medtner can be charged.

It was said some years ago of Grieg, by a critic who would have preferred to see the Norwegian discard his accustomed Scandinavian idiom for a more universal method of expression, that he " never left the fjords." To judge from the latest published work, the three pieces, Opus 31, dedicated to the memory of that greatly gifted artist Stanchinsky (the sonata, Opus 30, is apparently still in manuscript), Medtner's inspiration is not slackening, despite his faithfulness to the keyboard. But the better one knows this splendid artist the more one feels that until he forsakes the piano we shall never penetrate into the depths of his inner musical personality. No one could doubt for an instant that were Medtner to avail himself of orchestral colour the world would be made the richer by symphonic works which would arouse as great an enthusiasm as the symphonies of Brahms, without yielding anything to them in purity, and which would, one imagines, have a greater power to stir the emotions of the contemporary music-lover. The Russian musical world is justly proud of Medtner; whether the far greater things expected of him will be forthcoming appears to depend on whether he chooses to continue so to confine himself to his own instrument.

TCHEREPNIN

CHAPTER IX

TCHEREPNIN

(1)

WHEN, as a young man, Pushkin wrote his famous poem, *Russlan and Ludmilla,* the work upon which Glinka's opera of that name is founded, the poet's first essay in folk-art was accepted by many, whose acquaintance with the characteristics of native folk-lore was but limited, as fulfilling in every respect the nationalistic purpose for which Pushkin had intended it. By a later generation it was recognized as having many features testifying to its writer's close study of Lodovico Ariosto ; this circumstance finds its musical parallel in the now apparent Italianisms of Glinka's *A Life for the Tsar,* present also in a lesser degree in his other opera.

There are a number of tentative musical essays in folk-style to be discovered in the annals of Russian Opera, some of them occurring prior to the Glinkist era, but it is in orchestral and instrumental music that this kind of material can best be examined, since, in the smaller canvas, it occupies the whole area and is not merely episodical or ornamental. If one selects one figure alone from the multitude of personages peopling the fantastic territory of Russian folk-lore—that, for instance, of the forbidding witch Baba-Yaga —three works in which her horrible features and fearsome character are drawn spring at once to ᵗʰe mind : the orchestral pieces of Dargomijsky ᵃⁿd Lyadof and the piano " picture " in Moussorgsky's famous suite.

There has recently been painted a further portrait of the iron-beaked hag—the work of the subject of this chapter. As in the case of literature, the legendary style in Russian music has only been established after many efforts and much groping on the part of composers. And of all of those who have experimented, the first to succeed was Rimsky-Korsakof. To him we are indebted for the foundation of the musical language of Russian legendary-lore, and he, also, has left a literature abundant as to quantity and distinguished as to quality. Through him the fantastic became a predominating element in Russian music. For the vein he struck a name has been coined which hints at the substance of the tales he tells—a name derived from the rank or station of the ubiquitous heroine of Russian Legend : it is " Tsarevnism."

Tcherepnin, whose reputation was made by his musico-dramatic studies in mediævalism and mythology, *The Pavilion of Armida* and *Narcissus*, belongs to a younger generation, and the musical

TCHEREPNIN.

path he has cut for himself through the thick undergrowth of present-day Russian musical tendencies is apparently that which leads to a tonal presentment of these legends suitable for the modern ear. Seemingly Tcherepnin's purpose is that of interpreting Russian Legend to the outside world by means of music, for in selecting his musical material he has availed himself of substance which is not always Russian ; its suitability would appear to lie in that it is modern.

In the days of the fight for nationalism in Russian music there were several distinguished composers who dissented from Balakiref's creed ; they refused to tie themselves down to the native historical subject, adorned with folk-episodes, and claimed the right to choose both the inspiration, the matter and the manner of their works from the region whose product best corresponded with their creative mood. This group, usually associated with Moscow musical life, called itself the " Eclectics " and one of its foremost figures was Tchaikovsky. Some later works of Tcherepnin entitle one to suppose that an eclecticism of another kind is being adopted by him in the cause of nationalism. In his more recent output we observe many examples of which Russian legendary lore is the literary basis ; but their musical substance contains a number of elements peculiarly varied in nature. Music which frequently recalls

s

the composer's teacher—the prophet of "Tsarevn-ism "—which contains instrumental characteristics associated with Tchaikovsky and harmonic reminiscences of the French impressionists, of Strauss, and even of Schoenberg, and rivals at times the boldness of Stravinsky, may well be reckoned likely to catch the ear of Western Europe, and if by this means the claim of the Russian people—that the proper study of the Western European is Russia—can be substantiated, then Tcherepnin's eclecticism will have been worth while.

(2)

Nicholas Nicholaevich Tcherepnin was born in Petrograd in 1873. Destined for a legal career, he studied at Petrograd University ; whilst there he appears to have had an inkling of what the future had in store for him, and during the latter part of this period, which terminated in 1895, he was being taught by Rimsky-Korsakof, who had received him in his class at the Conservatoire. At this time he composed his first published work, a set of six songs. Showing great promise he was introduced, by his teacher, towards the end of the 'nineties, into the Belayef Circle (he left the Conservatoire in 1898), and attracting the sympathetic attention of the great publisher, who purchased the songs above-mentioned and other compositions, was appointed a year or two later as one of the conductors of the Russian Symphony Concerts, originally founded by Belayef. This position he still holds, in conjunction with a professorship at the Petrograd Conservatoire.

During his association with Belayef he came in contact with many musicians of repute, some of them having previously been his fellow-students in Rimsky-Korsakof's class; among these were Akimenko, Zolotaref, Sokolof and Wihtol; others, such as Arensky, Grechaninof, Taneyef and his pupil Skryabin, were already well-known in the musical world — the last-mentioned having recently been given a footing on the threshold of his remarkable career by Belayef.

Rimsky - Korsakof, as a teacher, resembled Taneyef, in that he strove to cultivate the individuality of his pupils. But Tcherepnin's earlier music, which at times rather sharply mirrors his teacher's musical countenance, tells us less of his own individuality than of a sympathetic attitude towards that of several other composers.

Together with this eclecticism in relation to material, Tcherepnin has shown catholicity in regard to form. His output does not invite close comparison in this respect with that of Rebikof, for in Tcherepnin's case the material compels the adoption of the chosen mould. He has entered almost every department of musical composition, and if he has so far refrained from the use of the legitimate musico-dramatic art-form of opera, the variety of conception displayed in his ballets proves him to be something more than a composer of the conventional choreographic example. In addition to the two ballets which brought him world - wide fame, *The Pavilion of Armida* and *Narcissus*, he has produced in the present year a work which should one day command a sympathetic attention in English-speaking countries, since this choreodrama is founded on Edgar Allan Poe's lurid story, *The Masque of the Red Death*. In the purely symphonic sphere he has composed a little Gavotte for small orchestra, the Prelude to Rostand's celebrated *Princesse Lointaine*, a symphonic poem describing the Witches' scene in *Macbeth*, a dramatic fantasia based on Tioutchef's *From Land to Land* and the orchestral sketch on the subject of the Fire-bird story, of which another version has been given us by Stravinsky. A number of choruses, with and without orchestra, also stand to his credit. He has written nearly fifty songs, among which should be specially mentioned the group entitled *From Hafiz*, the two series of Fairy Tales, settings of Balmont's *Children's Songs*, and the striking Ballad, *The Trumpet Sound*, to Merejkovsky's poem;

for piano there are the six illustrations to Pushkin's story, *The Fisherman and the Fish*, which won
him the Glinka Prize of three hundred roubles in
1913, under the scheme endowed by Belayef, the
piano Concerto, similarly honoured four years
previously, and the delightful series of fourteen
sketches giving a musical representation of the
illustrations in Benois' *Alphabet in Pictures*. To
the literature of chamber-music he has contributed only the string quartet, Opus 11, and his
examples for the orchestral instruments are at
present limited to two violin pieces and a series
of six quartets for four horns. Conspicuously
absent from this list is the symphony pure and
simple ; Tcherepnin's first piece of abstract music
in this form has only lately been completed. While
lovers of chamber-music may feel a little disap-
pointed that the composer's association with the
Belayef group was not more productive in this
matter, they will concede that Tcherepnin, on
the showing of a list of his works, can claim to be
a fairly versatile composer.

(3)

Thanks to the establishment of the Russian
Ballet in the favour of British theatre-goers, we
were given a timely opportunity of hearing the
two works which at the moment of their production were typical of Tcherepnin. A return to the

score of the first shows as plainly as possible what
has been, and indeed still seems to be, its author's
relation to Russian music. In treating this subject (*The Pavilion of Armida*) he might well have
illustrated it by music belonging wholly to its
literary period, that of Louis XIV. But if, years
ago, we did not recognize the echoes of Delibes
(the early Gavotte for orchestra is a louder one)
it was because that style seemed fairly fitted for
the subject; if we were not sensible of Wagnerian
effects, the cause of our deafness to them may have
been that we had too recently emerged from
an era when, to many, dramatic music meant
Wagnerian music; and as to our having ignored
the very evident influence of Tchaikovsky, that
is easily explained when we remember that the
Tchaikovskian manner stood in those days for the
Russian, and may have been accepted as belonging
equally to Tcherepnin. To find evidence of these
influences, and that of Rimsky-Korsakof, one need
go no further than the Introduction, which
furnishes convincing examples of each.

The last-named influence is, as it were, fundamental, and apparently, abiding. It may be
traced not only in Tcherepnin's occasional excur-
sions into " Tsarevnism," such as *The Enchanted
Garden*, but in the more direct nationalism of the
Old Song, Opus 6, No. 2, for chorus, which has a
folk-song character and refers to Ivan the Terrible,

Kazan and the Tatars (it is dedicated to Rimsky-Korsakof) ; it is seen even in the recent *Masque of the Red Death*. But before that it might have been recognized in *Narcissus*. In the music to this adaptation of Ovid's poem the harmonic effects were well calculated to please us ; they reflect the style of the French impressionists, and were, so to say, in the " modern " vogue at that particular moment at which we were beginning to feel that this method of expressing emotion in music was the most effective imaginable. But the Korsakovian manner, which now shared, with the dramatic realism and the musical laconicism of Moussorgsky, the burden of representing the newly-discovered Russian musical character, was here again present, betraying itself chiefly in figuration—as, for instance, in the Bacchante's Dance, and in that also of Narcissus—but occasionally in the scoring as well. Had it been possible to look into the future it would perhaps have been realized that Tcherepnin's power of cultivating the germs of successive modern musical ideas was bringing him dangerously near the position of poor Echo, his heroine.

(4)

The comparison made by a Russian, when discussing Tcherepnin's last contribution to the stage, *The Masque of the Red Death,* tempts one to prolong the metaphor. " Tcherepnin," observes Mr. Glinsky, in an article on this choreodrama, " may well be compared to Poe's hero." " The tastes of the duke " (Prince Prospero), says the American, " were peculiar. He had a fine eye for colours and effects. He disregarded the *decora* of mere fashion." But if, as it would appear, the Russian critic thinks that Tcherepnin's employment of devices which are not of his own devising is to be characterized as a well-meaning attempt to make of Russian music " an organic confluence of divers musical elements," he must, when drawing this analogy, have forgotten that although the first part of his quotation is well applied, the second is somewhat wide of the mark ; for, while, in *The Masque of the Red Death,* Tcherepnin would apparently have us believe that the harmonic experiments he has made therein are additions of permanent value to Russian music, the truth is that they are of an importance entirely transitory. His worst mistake, which consists in the harmonization of a whole dance according to the tonal-scale system, seems a very telling example of the misguided emphasis of an accessory. The presence of features which have been brought, either consciously or otherwise, into the harmonic and rhythmic scheme, assists a little when they are manipulated by such a master of the orchestra as

Tcherepnin, and if, also, they are introduced in a fashion that will make them appear the most suitable material for the action, emotion, or characterization to be emphasized in the music at a given moment. But Tcherepnin is too prone to plan his music—even when it belongs to this type, in which the stage movement demands full consideration—as a musician and not as a musico-dramatist. Therein lies his greatest danger. The public is by no means averse from hearing music that recalls other music, but one imagines that unless they are suitably applied, both as to material and dimension, these reminiscences will not win the full measure of favour. The story of *The Masque of the Red Death* is one which presents many features attractive to musicians, but its successful setting requires music that is evoked by the tremendously enthralling tale itself, music which is inspired by the decorative colour and the picturesque episodic material, but above all by the horror experienced in the anticipation of the doom of Prince Prospero and his guests.

(5)

In his symphonic music—chiefly, as has been stated, of the programmatic order—Tcherepnin evinces the same mastery of orchestral effect. Since the work is dedicated to Glazounof, one would expect the treatment of the Cave Scene (Act IV) of *Macbeth*, Opus 12, to be in accordance with that master's views of the function of programme music, but Tcherepnin has dealt in detail with its highly dramatic occurrences. At certain moments, such as the passage which occurs at the Second Apparition's words : " laugh to scorn the power of man, for none of woman born shall harm Macbeth," we discern the influence of Tchaikovsky, of whose rushing scale passages Tcherepnin seems particularly fond, but one cannot deny that in this as well as in other cases the material is both well-chosen and ably handled.

In the Dramatic Fantasia, *From Land to Land*, Opus 17, there are signs that the budding fame of Skryabin has not been without its effect on this observer of current tendencies, and although there is little yet to suggest the fourth-chords of *The Masque*, the second theme appears to mirror the melodic manner of the composer of the *Poem of Ecstasy* ; but there are clear evidences not only in this respect but in the scoring that the fascination of Tchaikovsky—who might well have designed the plunges of strings and clarinets at certain dramatic points—has not been dissipated.

In *The Enchanted Garden*, Opus 39, an orchestral suite, the composer is said to have reached the apogee of " Tsarevnism." According to Mr. Tiounayef, the contemplation of Kashchei's garden has evoked music that is " Korsakovian," both in kind and in the manner of its application. Tcherepnin follows the plan of *The Tale* and of *Sheherazade* in avoiding close description, but, apparently, the requisite enchantment is achieved in the " wonderful harmonic texture and exquisite orchestration, fresh, a little whimsical, but expressive."

In the arrangement of his orchestral material, in the cultivation of the fruits of his eclecticism, Tcherepnin reveals an originality that is not, as may be gathered, conspicuous in thematic and harmonic matters. Of instrumentation and of orchestration he is really a master. He does not seem to have been called by any of his champions or critics what he obviously is—a composer whose creative medium is, properly speaking, orchestral effect. The ideas which he borrows are rarely if ever commonplace, and even the music of so early a work as the *Princesse Lointaine*, thanks to its innate distinction, does not sound as old-fashioned as many pieces of that type and period ; one is almost persuaded that Tcherepnin's orchestral gift would enable him to transform the banal into something quite distinguished.

To obtain a desired effect he is prepared to go to considerable lengths ; of this the scoring of *The Masque* affords abundant proof. To a heavy " quintet " and an augmented wind department, he adds, besides the now popular celeste, a big array of percussion and " effects," which include mandoline, zither, gusli, metallophone and other instruments not often seen in the dramatic orchestra. The mandoline recalls Mahler, but its part in this instance is not that of rendering appropriate incidental music ; it is a contrivance whereby a particular tone-colour may be obtained ; combined with other instruments, it produces the sound of the striking clock, and if one can judge from the piano's rendering of the heavy chords *Molto sostenuto, quasi adagio,* which interrupt the furious dance of Prospero's guests, and the sharp beat of the treble note that follows them, the mandoline and gusli should be capable of good service in the reproduction of the " clear and loud and deep and exceedingly musical " sound which came from the " brazen lungs of the clock."

(6)

The love of orchestral effect brings certain disadvantages in its train. Tcherepnin's later piano pieces and songs are not pianistic in quality. In the earlier vocal works the figuration of his accompaniments reveals a noticeable lack of invention, and in such numbers as the Tolstoi song (Opus 1), Lermontof's " They loved one another " (Opus 22), the Maikof example (Opus 21), and the fourth

of the *From Hafiz* set, the piano is given music
which has a structural form common to these and
others, and is strictly conventional in idea. There
is also noticeable in this class of work an addiction
to harp passages which robs them of variety, when
considered collectively.

Nothing more clearly demonstrates Tcherepnin's orchestral method of thought than the
frequency with which he is obliged to call in the
aid of a third stave, both in songs and piano
pieces. In one of the six preludes which bear
the same Opus number as the Dramatic Fantasia
for orchestra, he uses four, and in the elaborate
cadenza of the piano Concerto, in which the solo
instrument appears to be enjoying its freedom
after a period of restraint—there are no less than
seven ! This work, like that of his master, which
was dedicated to Liszt, is in one continuous movement.

In two works of recent date, however, Tcherepnin contrives to bring about a crystallization of
elements. In his delightful setting of the Balmont
Fairy Tales he has reached something like a style
of his own, and there is a conciseness of form and
a harmonic economy which suit the literary
material admirably. This series, which should
become exceedingly popular examples of music
for the child, consists of a number of nursery
songs. Their titles, which include *The Hare*,

Nonsense Story, Spanish Cradle-Song—a particularly charming work—and *Pansies,* suggests a more homely fantasticism than that of the *Enchanted Garden,* and this is fully borne out by the simple though pungent music.

A more remarkable series, and one containing music of somewhat greater complexity, is that of the fourteen sketches for Alexandre Benois' Russian Alphabet. Roughly speaking, these come within the same category as Moussorgsky's monument to Hartmann. But here the musician has to deal with material that is partly comic, partly grotesque, and he does so in a fittingly objective manner. The series is divided into two suites. Contained in these are the Arab, who " patters " before the curtain of a booth at a country fair, the General, a boy conducting lead soldiers in an attack upon a cardboard fortress (set to mock-martial music), the Stars, a picture of the learned men who gave astronomical information to the courtiers of the Empress Elizabeth, a Witch enticing children into her gingerbread house (a suggestion here of the Fairy Sugar-plum of the *Nut-Cracker* suite), children in a furrier's shop frightened at a stuffed bear, and other subjects which are treated in so fascinating a manner as to make one doubtful whether the mental images they conjure up are not perhaps preferable to a sight of Benois' original.

Tcherepnin

To the supposition that Tcherepnin's future musical habitation is to be found in the domain of fantastic legend, colour is lent by the content of one of his latest works, the six musical illustrations to Pushkin's *Fisherman and the Fish*. These, although dedicated " To my dear son, Sasha," do not belong to the nursery, where tales with a moral are detested. But in them the Russian child of to-day will presently find a specimen of nationalistic music, which, though rooted in the soil of the mid-nineteenth century movement, has nothing in it that too closely resembles the somewhat primitive musical nationalism then favoured. *The Fisherman and the Fish* is modern music, but is full of veiled allusions to the land which is made the story's new home by Pushkin.

It is in such works as this that Tcherepnin joins forces with Stravinsky and becomes a very valuable acquisition to Russian musical society. The nationalism of the Fairy Tales and of the Pushkin example is perhaps a shade subtler than that of *Petroushka*, and one component that contributes to this subtlety is that the music is not wholly of Slavonic origin. In *The Fisherman and the Fish* are the trumpet fanfares that were introduced by Rimsky-Korsakof in his opera, *The Legend of Tsar Saltan*, and are by way of becoming a conventionalized musical device of Russian musical fantasy (they symbolize a return to the region of the

271

fantastic) ; but the *Spanish Cradle Song* (from the Balmont series) in which Tcherepnin emphasizes the Oriental harmonic characteristics of the music of Spain rather than its peculiar rhythmical features—thus creating a connection with Russian music less obvious but more abiding—is one of many evidences of an enlightened eclecticism. Works of this kind are just now particularly welcome. We have learned, as Borodin hinted we should, that Russians are not quite the people we thought them, that they have a livelier appreciation of the arts than we. That appreciation is the fruit as much of the arts themselves as of the Russian character. The Russian's love of the legendary and the fantastic has been fostered by successive generations of artists. Of late years we have been given a glimpse of this region of fantasy and legend. But we have had to go for it to the theatre. If Tcherepnin, as seems likely, intends to devote himself in the future to the popularization of the form adopted in the *Fairy Tales* and *The Alphabet*, he will provide for us an opportunity of obtaining a deep insight into the Russian character through an easily accessible means. In thus occupying himself he should win an esteem more permanent than that brought him by his ballets.

GRECHANINOF

CHAPTER X

GRECHANINOF

(1)

AMONG lovers of vocal and chamber-music, the description of Grechaninof as a creative artist who cannot claim a place among the stars of the first magnitude may perhaps cause a little surprise, and possibly some resentment. His name is well known, and his list of works is of imposing dimensions and well-varied, including examples of opera, symphony, chamber, solo-instrumental and vocal music, many sacred choruses, etc. He displays a decided catholicity in his literary tastes in the choice of texts from such poets as Ostrovsky, Koltsof, A.Tolstoi, Tioutchef, Baudelaire, Brioussof, Maeterlinck, Balmont and Merejkovsky, and a keenness in searching for fresh and interesting thematic material is manifested by the treatment of Scottish, Mossulman and Bulgarian melodies.

It is not always safe to rely upon the judgments on native music which reach us from Russia, because the acrimony of the disputes of the 'sixties and 'seventies has not altogether disappeared ; most musicians are prepared to adopt an unbiassed attitude towards each aspect of contemporary Russian music, but they are still

275

occasionally goaded into active protest by writers who naïvely deprecate every symptom of progress, still wielding the shaft of a twigless besom even against " programme music," condemning the music of Skryabin, Stravinsky, Rebikof, and Tcherepnin with the one comprehensive epithet " noise," censuring Rakhmaninof for his experiment in " Kouchkism," putting up prayers that Glazounof may never have a return of his erstwhile nationalist sympathies, and, presumably for want of a more explicit deprecation of Medtner's misdeeds, mis-spelling his surname!

(2)

In Grechaninof's case, however, there is less ground for suspicion of bias. In two senses he belongs to both schools, for on the one hand he completed in Petrograd the musical education begun in Moscow, and on the other he has been a fairly successful nationalist and is now experimenting in " impressionism."

In the circumstances, then, one feels justified in quoting, in support of one's own contention, the opinion expressed not long since by a Petrograd writer who unhesitatingly placed Grechaninof " in the category of the ' *dii minores* ' of our Olympus," averring that the performance of a number of compositions in succession (a Grechaninof programme) was a mistake, and that presented in this way the composer's product seemed less interesting than it actually is.

The fact seems to be that while Grechaninof has been influenced by both schools, his individuality is not sufficiently strong to contribute any strikingly original conceptions in support of their artistic propaganda. As a nationalist he has indulged mildly in the use of the folk-theme, as in the first symphony (written in 1894 and dedicated to Rimsky-Korsakof), which shows also, in the Finale, some indebtedness to Borodin ; a further evidence of " Kouchkist " sympathies is the employment of a subject from the Vladimir Cycle in the opera, *Dobrinya Nikitich*. As an " eclectic " he is not particularly convincing ; his setting of Baudelaire's *Fleurs de Mal* reveals something less than a full appreciation of the poet : the vision of *splendeur orientale* evokes a musical expression which seems to fall between the Slavonic and the Latin conception of such an allurement. As to the second quartet, Opus 70, which appears to be an attempt to keep abreast of the times, it contains some odder contrasts than that observed by a critic on its performance in manuscript—the presence of a somewhat scholastic *fugato* passage in the Largo—for its Finale is curiously out of character with its first and third movements, and the work as a whole is apparently inspired from two diverse sources, the one original and the other, in the personal sense, foreign. On the whole we may counsel those who would know Grechaninof at his best, and ,as a composer possessing great distinction, to seek acquaintance with the songs of his middle and later period. Among these they will find examples just as deserving of popularity as *Triste est le Steppe* and rather more in harmony with our present wider view of the Russian character.

(3)

Alexander Tikhonovich Grechaninof was born at Moscow on October 13th, 1864. His father, who came of a mercantile family, did not look upon music as an essential feature of the curriculum of primary education ; thus the boy's first practical experience of the art was delayed until he was thirteen years of age, when a piano was purchased for his sister, who belonged to a sex privileged in this particular, and on this instrument he began to pick out melodies and, later, chords. The future composer had, however, already displayed the inclination for sacred music which became marked in later days, and this was discerned by his mother, whose strength of character rendered her a powerful ally when it became necessary to overcome the father's stern opposition to the youngster's preoccupation with music. This had to be faced when, after giving way to his son's desire to substitute a classical for a commercial education, Tikhon Gerassimovich learned of the havoc threatening his plans, wrought by an evening of chamber-music, which, so it appears, had the effect of strengthening our subject's resolve to enter the musical profession.

When, in his seventeenth year, young Alexander became a pupil at the Conservatoire, his father regarded the step as one likely to bring a blemish upon the family records.

Grechaninof's first teacher was Kashkin ; later he entered Safonof's piano class, studying counter-point, at first with Laroche, who proved to be an unsatisfactory teacher, and afterwards with Hubert. His experience in the harmony and form classes of Arensky was even more disconcerting than the neglect of Laroche, for Arensky bluntly confessed himself incapable of discovering in his pupil any special aptitude, thus showing his usual lack of discernment.

(4)

Completely discouraged the student determined to seek instruction elsewhere, and after a few months' study with Taneyef, the benefits of which were subsequently acknowledged in the dedica-tion of the piano trio, he betook himself to Petro-grad, entering its Conservatoire in the autumn term of 1890.

Here, under the kindly tutorial care of Rimsky-Korsakof, the disenchanted Muscovite began to prepare for a graduation in " nationalism."

During the three years spent in this sympathetic environment he succeeded in winning the friendship of his teacher and in furnishing proofs of his conversion to " Kouchkism." One does not include among these an examination exercise, the cantata *Samson*, for solo voice, chorus and orchestra, apparently the first of his works to be publicly performed (1893) ; but the string quartet, Opus 2, which won a prize offered by the Petrograd Chamber Music Society and was produced in 1894, and the acceptance by Rimsky-Korsakof of the dedication " as a token of profound esteem and recognition " of the first symphony, composed in the same year, may be taken as satisfactory evidence.

Grechaninof, having remained six years in Petrograd, where he had made a brave effort to support himself by teaching, was at length obliged, through considerations of finance, to return to Moscow.

Two of his larger works were undertaken soon after settling down in his native city. The first, the opera *Dobrinya Nikitich* (Opus 22), begun under Kouchkist influence in 1895, and resumed some years later at the instigation of Stassof, was not performed until 1903, when, after a concert

GRECHANINOF.

production by Count Sheremetief, it was staged at the Great Theatre and achieved a success which is sometimes attributed to the presence of the " fashionable " Shalyapin in the cast.

(5)

Meanwhile Grechaninof had begun to lay the foundation of his repute as a composer of sacred music, writing a number of devotional works and proclaiming by means of newspaper articles a determination to revive the somewhat flagging spirituality of this class of music. This brought him in friendly contact with Smolensky, then the director of the Moscow Synodal School.

His interest in this branch of his art did not, however, altogether divert his attention from its secular side. The music to the *Snow-Maiden* of Ostrovsky, originally commissioned by the directors of the recently founded Moscow Art Theatre, was produced in September, 1900, but served only to provoke unfavourable comparisons with Tchaikovsky and Rimsky-Korsakof, whose opera on the subject is generally reckoned a *magnum opus*; a second symphony (in A minor), the piano trio (Opus 38), the music to A. Tolstoi's trilogy of the *Troublous Times* (first two parts), and a further opera on Maeterlinck's *Sœur Béatrice* (1909-10) followed, the latter being staged in the winter of 1913-14, only to be removed from the repertoire after four performances, owing to the Censor's objection to the dramatic impersonation of the Virgin. *Sœur Béatrice* is pronounced to be a work having much musical beauty and constructed on sound lines ; in the latter particular it appears to be a great advance on *Dobrinya Nikitich*. A curious feature of the former work is its employment of themes already used in the setting of Baudelaire, in which the composer has pursued the unusual course of relying upon two contrasted principal themes which recur in the music of the *Fleurs de Mal*.

With the exception of the chamber examples, the above-mentioned works being, for the amateur, mostly of an inaccessible kind, cannot contribute to his formation of a judgment on their composer. Fortunately, however, Grechaninof has written a host of songs ; in them he has provided material suitable for all tastes, and, perhaps, in view of his having specified that some of his child-songs are for " elder children," one may also say for all ages ! In his numerous children's songs—the best-known are those in the series of ten, entitled *Snowflakes*, Opus 47—there are frequent allusions to folk-lore and song, which render them highly suitable for their destined purpose, while the accompaniments are devoid of any complexity. Simplicity also distinguishes some later specimens, particularly those in the series Opus 66, in which *The Bells*, No. 5, consists of a specified quotation from national song.

In the very beautiful *Five Poems*, under the collective title of *Ad Astra*, Opus 54, the piano writing is richer, to meet the requirements of the somewhat more emotional quality of the text, but the latest vocal works, inspired by the poet Ivanof (composed in 1915), reveal that when Grechaninof expresses himself simply his language does not lose but gains in impressiveness. Such a song as *Christ Arose*, from Opus 73, contains the latter quality in a high degree and suggests that the composer's success here is possibly due to his experience in writing sacred music.

One would like to think that Grechaninof is conscious of having " found himself " in works of this order ; his search has been long, but here are signs that it has been crowned with success, for Ivanof's Triptych is set to music that interprets the poet's mysticism faithfully, and that without a superfluous note.

Thus we may close our account of Grechaninof with a further reference to his compatriots' opinion, and echo the words of Kashkin, who, in 1908, numbered him among the composers from whom " much may be expected."

THE YOUNGER GENERATION

CHAPTER XI

THE YOUNGER GENERATION

(1)

IT would be pardonable to anticipate that the wonderful age which began with Glinka must one day draw to a close, to be then succeeded by an era of musical activity somewhat less inspiring to the chronicler. That day is apparently still far distant.

The claim that Russia should be given pride of place among the musical nations of the world is easily substantiated by reference to the immediate past. A glance along the ranks of living Russian composers will reveal many artists who are capable of producing a work that would bring them into a greater prominence, men who have already done a great deal to contribute, both in the pedagogic and the creative sphere, to the consolidation of the position so thoroughly well earned and so proudly held by Russian music. A glimpse into the future —to be obtained by an examination of the output of the younger men—leads one firmly to believe that Russia is not likely for many a generation to yield her priority.

We shall draw attention in the present chapter

287

to the young musicians on whom Russia will surely depend for her musical welfare in the next few decades. But before entering upon this undertaking it would be as well that the reader should be assisted to appreciate that between the men who have for various reasons been dealt with at length in the preceding chapters, and the younger generation, of whose representatives we shall presently give an account, there are a number of composers—some of them teachers also—who are doing or have accomplished sterling work in the consolidation of the Russian School. Were we to omit from this volume the names of such as Kastalsky, the Director of the Moscow Synodal School, Glière, the Principal of the Conservatoire at Kief, Vassilenko, the conductor, Akimenko, Catoire and Senilof, all of whom have distinguished themselves in the various spheres of musical composition, it would be difficult to understand how the link between the group formed by the distinguished composers already dealt with in the foregoing pages, and the younger men, is constituted. The musicians mentioned above have all had a share in the great constructive work of solidifying the wonderful edifice of which Glinka laid the foundation.

The first-named, although little known to us, has been by no means the least active. The presence of his name in a section styled "The

Younger Generation" requires explanation. Alexander Dmitrievich Kastalsky was born in 1856, at Moscow. He has been an assiduous worker, but his splendid labours in the field of sacred music have only recently received acknowledgment, and in his sixtieth year he saw himself acclaimed in an article of which the sardonic heading was " Discovery of Kastalsky." He received his musical education at the Moscow Conservatoire, his teachers there being Tchaikovsky, Hubert and Taneyef. He graduated in 1882, and five years later was appointed teacher at the Moscow Synodal School, of which institution he is now the much-respected head. The School was founded in 1886 for the training of singers for Church choirs.

It will be remembered that it was Glinka's desire that when listening to the type of opera to which he intended his *Life for the Tsar* to conform, his countrymen should " feel at home." It has been maintained in these pages that Stravinsky is imbued by a similar spirit. The " Reflections " of the Procurator of the Holy Synod, K. P. Pobiedonostsef, would have us believe that " the essential elements of religion are . . . involved with the psychical nature of a race," and a similar belief, but in respect of an accessory of religious service, is held by Kastalsky. He has been for years the head and front of a movement to re-establish Russian Church music on a foundation of Russian song. For this purpose he has long been a collector of folk-song, but it is only in recent years that he has begun to put his theories into practice in his own compositions. Yet by vigorous propaganda, in which his own writings have been a powerful agent, he has succeeded in encompassing what is termed a " restoration " of the music of the Church, which consists in something more than the introduction of the folk-song element. Kastalsky has aimed at a revitalization of Church music so that the spirit of worship shall be really contained in the music ; he desires to banish the mechanical, both in composition and rendering, to accomplish in fact for Church music what Rebikof, who has written on the subject in relation to sacred music, proposed to bring about in the secular domain : it is once again to become the language of the emotions. Kastalsky would introduce a profoundly emotional music into the Church service, and his arguments have carried conviction to such an extent that he has already a great following in Russia, one of his most successful disciples being Grechaninof.

To a long list of compositions he has lately added a much-praised *Requiem for the Fallen*. Here he seems to part company with the Procurator, for his work aims at a union of the Churches (from whose respective Liturgies he quotes), although only for the purpose of mourning the Allied victims of the war. No greater testimony could possibly be given to the success of his own application of his precepts than that provided by the participants who assure us that the effect of Kastalsky's Requiem was " congregational " in the sense that it exerted a tremendously moving power over everyone present, thus realizing, as more than one writer declared, the ideal at which Skryabin aimed in his " Mystery." Kastalsky speaks of his " restoration " as an " attempt," but the Requiem appears to have crowned this attempt with a very notable success.

(2)

Reinhold Morissovich Glière was born at Kief on January 11th, 1875. He entered the Moscow Conservatoire in 1894, was a pupil of Hrjimaly (for violin), Taneyef and Ippolitof-Ivanof, and completed his course in 1900. He remained for several years in the old capital, but was chosen in the autumn of 1914 as Director of the Conservatoire in his native city. This institution has since then gone through some vicissitudes, having to be removed during the evacuation of Kief to Rostof-on-Don, but since its return it has become, according to report, a very flourishing school.

Glière has composed some works of important dimensions for the orchestra. These include a symphony in E flat (Opus 8), a second in C minor (Opus 25), a symphonic poem, *Les Sirènes* (Opus 33) and a work (Opus 42) which is called a symphony, but is in reality the musical rendering of a series of episodes from the Vladimir Cycle relating to the folk-lore hero, Ilya of Murom. Glière has also written pieces for the component orchestral instruments individually (these include examples for violin, 'cello, double-bass, flute, clarinet, oboe, bassoon and horn) and in groups. His two string quartets, especially the second, have enjoyed a certain vogue ; the sextets and octet for strings, however, are not often played. There are a good many pieces for two pianos (Opp. 41 and 61), in which Glière contributes to a literature enlarged by Arensky and Rakhmaninof, and a large number of songs to texts of Koltsof, A. Tolstoi, Balmont—whose *Russalka* he has set for voice and orchestra—Ogaref, Apukhtin, Biely, F. Sologub and Makovsky.

Of all his works the last two symphonic examples are decidedly the most interesting. *Les Sirènes*, which is planned for a generous orchestra, makes an effort at descriptiveness of the fullest kind, but its composer, unlike the mariners he depicts, finds salvation, and not destruction, when listening to the song of Wagner and Debussy. In the other programmatic symphony, which has been performed by Mr. Dan Godfrey at Bournemouth,

Glière has adopted a fully nationalistic programme. Ilya the sleeper is awakened by the singing of the blind pilgrims; his conflicts with the Nightingale-Robber and the Tatars, the feast at Vladimir's Court, his conversion to Christianity and his final petrifaction are features which call to mind the epic-loving Borodin. Glière's music is said, in certain moments, to recall that of the composer of *Prince Igor*, but in places such as that in which the song of birds is prominent he becomes reminiscent, to us, of the Waldweben, to Russians of Skryabin's *Divine Poem*. The many fine climaxes demanded by the subject are, it appears, obtained by brilliancy rather than by rugged strength. Glière, a successful teacher, has yet to find his musical individuality; like Tcherepnin, he is a master of orchestral effect, but his harmonic conceptions exhibit no great originality.

(3)

Sergei Nikiforovich Vassilenko, famous as an organizer of concerts which are an important feature of musical life in Russia, has, as a creative musician, fallen under much the same influences as Glière. Born at Moscow in 1872, he was educated for the Law, but entered the Conservatoire in 1896, spending the next five years in the classes of Taneyef and Ippolitof-Ivanof. At the conclusion of his course he received the gold medal for his first important composition, a Cantata, since dramatized, on the subject of Rimsky-Korsakof's spiritual opera, *The Legend of Kitej*. Some of the Russian critics have entered so deeply into the controversy as to priority in the choice of this subject as to have forgotten the primary intention of discussing the merits of Vassilenko's work, but Cheshikin, when dealing with it on its production as an opera in 1903, by Ippolitof-Ivanof, attributes its fantastic colour and other features to Rimsky-Korsakof and its epic style to Borodin, giving chapter and verse in support of his verdict.

Mediævalism was soon discarded, but the evidence of Kouchkist sympathies remains, the Adagio of the second symphony again recalling Rimsky-Korsakof. But in this work Vassilenko has emerged from a period of which the symphonic suite, *Au Soleil*, is representative. This latter might well have been inspired by Henri Fabre; its "literary" foundation certainly suggests a familiarity with the insect world, and its music, introduced to us by Sir Henry Wood in 1913, seemed then to have been intended as a compliment to some of the eminent entomologist's countrymen. In the second symphony, however, there is a great advance; the orchestral mastery is maintained, and on the whole the harmonic method, which owes something to certain progressive contemporaries, is not a little

individual. Another recent work is *The Witches'*
Flight, inspired by passages from Merejkovsky's
Resurrection of the Gods.

Vassilenko has written some choice songs and
the composition of a *War March* is recorded.

(4)

A Little-Russian origin is again suggested by
the name of Fedor Akimenko, and, by his music,
French sympathies more pronounced than those
of Vassilenko. He was born at Kharkof on
February 8th, 1876, but at the age of ten was sent
to the Imperial Chapel, Petrograd, then under the
direction of Balakiref, who conceived a great liking
for the youngster. But despite this early contact
with one in the direct line of nationalist tradition,
Akimenko, although a prolific composer, has
apparently written little that can be regarded as
the outcome of a desire to emulate the leader of
the Kouchka. During a sojourn in France he
came under the influence of some neo-Impression-
ists whose manner he has cleverly reproduced in
a large number of piano pieces. He has written a
good many songs, some of them of considerable
charm, and solo-instrumental pieces. In many of
these, although the idiom is French, there is an
underlying individuality in the manipulation of
the medium, and, on the whole, Akimenko can

fairly be styled a composer who is always refined and never commonplace.

" Were the Russian musical family without its Akimenko," says a compatriot, " we should be the poorer for a very gifted artist." His larger compositions include a B minor symphony and a *Poem-Nocturne* for orchestra, inspired by Lermontof's *Angel*; like Glière, he has written much for the individual instrument and has a 'cello concerto and a violin sonata to his credit.

Akimenko is at present a professor of theoretical subjects at Petrograd Conservatoire.

(5)

In George Catoire we have again a composer who owes his training to some extent to a nationalist teacher. But as in addition to his studies with Lyadof, Catoire can claim a Berlin education and a French parentage, one would expect to have some difficulty in tracing his musical origins. This expectation is realized on examination of his more recent songs, which have French texts and a vocal method which is apparently the outcome of German teaching. The selection of such subjects as those of the symphonic poem *Mtsyri*, based on Lermontof's famous poem, of the same poet's *Russalka* for a Cantata, and the music of his piano trio, Opus 14, which employs some

A. Krein.   Stanchinsky.   G. Krein.   Gunst.   Sabaneyef.

themes of folk origin, are reminders of a time when Catoire was inclined towards nationalism. But the maturer works, which include an ambitious piano quintet, Opus 28, settings of Verhaeren and Verlaine, Opus 22, and even the violin sonata, Opus 20, show him to be distinctly in sympathy with the older modern Frenchmen. At the same time Catoire's music preserves an individuality, and though not of a very accessible kind, has an attractiveness that requires only a sufficient acquaintance to make itself apparent. It is on account of this quality of obscurity that Catoire has been called a composer for musicians ; one might go further and say that he is, at times, like Medtner, a composer for players ; but, as will be obvious, a sufficient application on the part of the listener will serve in time to secure comprehension of any work, and one can declare with conviction that Catoire's music will repay such perseverance. In addition to the examples above-mentioned he has composed a symphony (Opus 7) and a piano concerto (Opus 21).

(6)

Lermontof's *Mtsyri* has found another musical interpreter in Vladimir Alekseyevich Senilof, born on July 27th, 1875, at Viatka. Of this composer it is only possible to judge at first hand by the quality of some excellent songs issued by Jurgen-son. Having written three operas, a like number of string quartets and four symphonic poems, one of which is that referred to above, Senilof remains unpublished, unacted, unperformed, but not un-sung, for his vocal works are by their success fully justifying the confidence of his publisher, as well they might, by their merit.

However, thanks to the championship of Mr. Tiounayef, one is able to gather some particulars of Senilof's career and of his work as a whole. During the period of his university course at Petrograd—he was a law-student—he was intro-duced to Rimsky-Korsakof, who examined some compositions and felt justified in recommending the youth to continue his musical education. Subsequently, acting on the advice of Sapelnikof, he went to Leipsic, attended Riemann's lectures on Æsthetics and took private lessons from that encyclopædist. Having assisted Riemann in some researches which resulted in the publication in 1909 of a volume on Byzantine music, he returned to Russia and studied composition and instru-mentation with Rimsky-Korsakof, remaining at the Conservatoire until 1906. Senilof is at present the Principal of a private music school.

To judge by the material of the operas described by Mr. Tiounayef, Senilof makes full use of a wide erudition, a strong musical gift and a

well-developed orchestral technique. Riemann
made of him a learned musician, and he improves
upon the methods of the founder of "Tsarevnism"
by using Arabian and Byzantine material when
the hero of his second opera, *Vassily Buslaef*, goes
on his pilgrimage to the Holy Land. In the first,
Gregory the Invincible, a kind of mystical " Act,"
his polyphonic mastery is given its opportunity,
while in the setting of Euripides' *Hippolytus* he
leans to the declamatory type of opera, in which
the interest lies in a musical dialogue. His songs
reveal him to be a composer by whom modernity
of method is not allowed to become obtrusive ;
he expresses his thoughts in spontaneous fashion
without seeking after novelty, but frequently
strikes a note which, although new, does not leave
an impression of strangeness but of a strongly felt
emotion. The three settings of Remizof, Opus
10, are early works, but are considered representative, and they may well be recommended, having
been provided with an English text by Mr.
Calvocoressi. Their diversity of style and design
and their distinction, both in the musical material
and its application, will serve to whet the appetite
of those who are susceptible to aristocratic refinement. The gratification of such an appetite is
apparently something that lies " on the knees " of
the publishers.

(7)

Turning to the youngest, to those who might well be called "twentieth-century composers," since most of them have revealed their creative gifts only within the last few years, we observe in the condition of Russian music symptoms of the utmost prosperity. In every department but one there are to be found composers who are not only well qualified to supply material that will uphold the reputation of musical Russia, but who are constantly seeking to enrich their art with new ideas, to revitalize it by frequent contact with the finest products of the sister arts. It should, perhaps, be emphasized that in this respect the musician has established a reciprocal understanding with the painter and the poet. In Russia, sympathy between painter and musician is a tradition, and to that we owe the fine portraits of all the representative composers since Glinka. With the exception of Chabrier, one cannot readily name a non-Russian composer who has shown so intelligent an appreciation of painting. At the present time we find in course of formation a complete *rapprochement* between Russian poets and musicians ; among the former Balmont, Ivanof, and latterly Remizof, have shown themselves capable of assisting in the exposition of the most progressive composers of the day.

In this way music has become more fully

representative of contemporary thought, and has gained, as an art, a dignity that is a little lacking in other countries where it is treated as a poor, and sometimes an importunate, relation of the plastic arts and literature. Another point worthy of attention is that the musician of the rising generation is as a rule well able to hold his own with the professional critic in wielding the pen in a literary capacity.

That native opera is the least thriving branch of music in Russia is due in part to the popularity of Ballet, but also to a tradition of managerial dilatoriness in production. The composition of opera is at the moment in the hands of the minor musicians, and, as a consequence, those which have been produced in the last few years, as, for instance, Kazanli's *Miranda*, Olenin's *Kudeyar*—a curious experiment which consists entirely of folk-song, the subject relating to the period of Stenka Razin—and A. S. Taneyef's *The Snowstorm*, have not succeeded in brightening the prospects of the operatic composer. Possibly, when Prokofief's setting of Dostoyevsky's *The Gambler* comes to be mounted there may be a revival which is very much overdue.

As this composer is the most discussed Russian musician of the day, and the most versatile, we may perhaps be allowed to ignore that he is one of the youngest.

Prokofief has been called the *enfant terrible* and the " young barbarian " of the Petrograd musical world; one writer wondered (in 1914) that this fair-haired and apparently inoffensive stripling should be capable of " such musical devilry " ; a little later he was referred to by a critic, who was dealing with his treatment of Andersen's *Ugly Duckling*, as in all probability the beautiful swan among Russian musicians of the future and " symptoms of genius " are observed by another. Even if we accept the verdict delivered after the production of the exceedingly provocative *Scythian Suite*, an estimate that necessitated the description of the composer as a " raging futurist," we shall do well to bear in mind that, as there is always a future to be reckoned with, and as there are always with us a number of folk who persist in denying this obvious fact, it behoves the futurist to rage ; the poor futurist knows only too well how painful a past the future has.

Sergei Prokofief was born in 1891 and studied at the Conservatoire, his teachers being Lyadof (for counterpoint and fugue), Annette Essipof (piano) and Tcherepnin. His first published work, a single-movement sonata in F minor, bears the date 1909, but this is not to be considered either as a first attempt or as being representative of the composer. Pre-dating this are two of the charming pieces forming the suite, Opus 12, for piano, which are revised versions of the work of a youth in the middle 'teens. The *Sinfonietta* for small orchestra, which belongs to the same year as the sonata, has also been subjected to a revision, but this, from all accounts, is a highly original work, a term which cannot be applied to the sonata. Between the latter and his next essay in that form lies, officially, so to speak, the suite, Opus 12, consisting of ten piano pieces composed at different times. Of these the numbers which reveal something of the nature of Prokofief's splendid genius are a delightful *Rigaudon* in C (1913), in which he proves that the ancient forms are capable of containing a modern composer's most individual expressions, a very charming *Legend* which hints at the harmonic blend (for which Mr. Karatigin revives the term *Heterophony*), later exploited in the *Scythian Suite*, and a brilliant *Prelude*. This is equally suited for a harp rendering ; the penultimate number, a *Humoristic Scherzo*, in imitation of four bassoons, leaves one in doubt as to whether it is intended for keyboard or reeds, a doubt which the quotation from Griboyedof—a humorous reference to the difficult articulation of the bassoon—does nothing to dispel. In the second sonata, Opus 14 (1912), Prokofief proceeds *à rebours*, forsaking the single-movement, also employed in the first piano concerto, Opus 10, for a four-part form ; but there is no mistaking the progress exhibited in its harmonic substance, though at times there is a little hesitation, as in the treatment of the second theme of the initial Allegro. A further concerto is very highly spoken of, but the work which has transformed Prokofief's fame into notoriety is the *Scythian Suite* for orchestra, Opus 20, entitled *Alla and Lolly*. This has been favourably compared with Stravinsky's *Rite of Spring* in all respects save orchestration, but a comparison which it is perhaps safer to quote is that made between the former and Borodin's Polovtsian Dances from *Prince Igor*. It is evident that its essentially musical quality constitutes the contrast between Prokofief's work and Stravinsky's, and its resemblance to Borodin's. The *Scythian Suite* is in four movements.

The predominant characteristic of Prokofief's manner is " puckishness," but this is toned down on occasion until it becomes the dry humour of a laconic old man. At the same time there is evidently an elemental and almost savage directness about the later works. The point emphasized by his champions is that at every situation he provides a new musical thought, and one writer marvels that a man brought up in the latter-day tradition of the Petrograd School should be able to write descriptive music that has all the picturesqueness of Rimsky-Korsakof's art and much of the delicacy of Lyadof's, and yet, while possessing

MYASKOVSKY.

these qualities, is entirely new and profoundly inspired.

(8)

" Myaskovsky's sonata is complex," says Prokofief, in a review of the work, " but those who are frightened away by its complexity will have ignored qualities such as nobility of material, carefulness of workmanship and a general attractiveness which render it one of the most interesting sonatas of recent times."

Like his eulogist, Nicholas Myaskovsky is also a literary man, and numbers among his writings a volume entitled *Beethoven and Tchaikovsky*. But there is in his musical work a strong link with his country's literature, for there are two examples, the symphonic poem *Alastor* (after Shelley) and a further orchestral piece based on Poe's " fable " *Silence*, which, but for Balmont's re-creations of these poets, would in all probability never have been written. Myaskovsky's musical personality is in complete contrast with that of Prokofief, but his origins, so far as his education is concerned, have something in common with those of his junior. The difference here is that Myaskovsky, who is a good deal older than his colleague, having been born in 1881, is a military engineer, and did not enter the Petrograd Conservatoire until a comparatively late age, when he became Prokofief's fellow-pupil in the classes of Annette Essipof and Lyadof. The contrast between the two as creative artists lies in that Myaskovsky is a deeply subjective composer, and is much less at home in the smaller forms. His music is sufficiently introspective in quality to have evoked comparison with that of Tchaikovsky. But between them there is a vast difference. Myaskovsky is subjective and introspective without being markedly personal. His gloom and even his pessimism are of a contemplative kind, his lyricism does not cloy.

In respect to form, Myaskovsky is no iconoclast; he has progressed from the three-section form of his first sonata to the continuous movement of the second—a profoundly poetic work, written in 1912—but that is at the present day to be considered a progression from an established classical to a conventionalized modern form, and such a circumstance would not justify astonishment at discovering that formal beauty is as great a feature of Myaskovsky's three symphonies as poetic content.

Even in his early work, of which the 'cello sonata, written in 1911, is a specimen, there is very little thematic resemblance to Tchaikovsky, and as the themes themselves were conceived at a still earlier date they would appear to warn us not to expect to find anything more than a qualified spiritual affinity between these composers.

The Younger Generation

Since his first mature work, *A Tale* for orchestra, he has drawn away from all physical influences (Wagner, Skryabin, and even Rakhmaninof are mentioned by Myaskovsky's appraisers), and in his third symphony—in two parts—although he remains like the first two, an "interior" artist, there is little enough to suggest a deficiency' in originality ; there are moments in the second part which recall Skryabin's melodic figuration, but as these have in the present instance been observed in a fragmentary thematic analysis, it would hardly be safe to set too much store by the qualities displayed by the themes when thus set forth.

In his songs, which are chiefly to the texts of " Z. Hippius " (Mme Merejkovsky), there is sufficient evidence of the composer's difficulty in limiting himself to so small a canvas. It cannot be said that he is " orchestral " ; there is, in fact, a deficiency of warmth. He has been compared with Moussorgsky (the *Without Sunlight* cycle is referred to), but the first " Hippius " series shows very little to justify that comparison ; when, however, he is taxed with writing, for the piano, music which accompanies neither the melody, the voice, nor the text " which he tries to illustrate," we understand that Myaskovsky is being blamed for conniving at the elevation of Song to a position of true artistic dignity.

Judging by his character as a musician one may safely expect that if Myaskovsky survives the great conflict in which, at the moment of writing, he is taking an active part, he will enrich the treasury of his country's music with further works inspired by a spirituality rendered still profounder.

(9)

As will be seen, Michael Gniessin is another composer whose product strengthens the link between art, literature and music. He was born at Rostof-on-Don in 1883, and received his musical education in the Petrograd Conservatoire, having for his teachers Rimsky-Korsakof and Glazounof. His compositions do not, however, reveal any sign of being influenced by these masters ; they are, in fact, singularly free from any suggestions of assimilated substance or manner. But they testify to a great depth of poetic feeling, and, further, to a technical mastery that is certainly not excelled by any other representative of young musical Russia. And he lacks nothing of the versatility of his contemporaries.

Curiously enough he has chosen, from the first days of his creative activity, to place himself in the debt of English literature. In Opus 3, No. 2 (written in 1908) he takes the text of the President's song from Pushkin's dramatic poem, *A*

The Younger Generation

Feast in Plague-Time, which the Russian poet
pretended to have founded upon a non-existent
tragedy (*The City of the Plague*) by " Christopher
North "; the slender symphonic fragment, *After
Shelley*, Opus 4 (1906), which was produced by
Siloti in 1908, has for its motto part of the
utterance of the Spirit of the Hour in Act III,
Scene 4, of *Prometheus Unbound*, and Beatrĭce's
song, " False Friend," from *The Cenci*, is the
subject of Opus 18. For these some of the credit
is obviously due to Balmont, who is no doubt
responsible for the version of the extract from
Poe's *Ligeia* which gives title and text to the
Poem for tenor and orchestra called *The Conqueror
Worm*, Opus 12.

But Gniessin is not backward in honouring the
poets of his own land, as is shown by his very
lovely songs embraced in the cycles *From Contemporary Poetry* (Balmont and Sologub), *Dedications* (Ivanof), and the same poet's *Rosarium* ; for
The Booth, a dramatic song, Opus 6 (1909), he is
indebted to Alexander Blok, and for this poet he
has provided the music of *Aliskan's Song* for the
drama, *Rose and Cross*. Painting receives its com-
memoration in the symphonic dithyramb, *Vroubel*,
Opus 8, which won Belayef's " Glinka " prize in
1913 ; it is dedicated to the great artist's wife, to
whom is also inscribed (in memory of this celebrated operatic singer) the Lament (Dedications,

No. 6), "Pale as death lies snow upon the meadow."

Gniessin forms in two ways a link with the Invincible Band. His music owes nothing to that Brotherhood, but he has invented a new form of vocalism which he calls " musical reading," and which " is not declamation . . . but reading with a precise observance of rhythm and pitch." This sufficiently explains itself, but we may emphasize its relation to the ideals of Dargomijsky. Gniessin has also rendered a service to the historian and the æsthetician as editor and introducer of Rimsky-Korsakof's literary articles, and as a lecturer on the subject of his master's pantheistic proclivities. As a song-writer, Gniessin has few equals.

Also associated with the memory of Rimsky-Korsakof is his son-in-law, Maximilian Steinberg, who edited the famous *Manual of Instrumentation*. Born at Vilna in 1883, he studied with Korsakof and Glazounof in the Petrograd Conservatoire. His manner bears a greater resemblance to the latter's than to that of his lamented father-in-law. One of his earliest works is an orchestral Fantasia described as " Dramatic," but that adjective certainly does not apply to the ballet *Midas*, performed at Drury Lane, one of three choreographic tableaux based on the *Metamorphoses* of Ovid. Steinberg has written two symphonies, the second of which, in B minor, has been heard in London, and a striking string quartet, Opus 5, a work which bears witness to craftsmanship rather than to inspiration, but despite his orchestral mastery he seems to be at his best in vocal examples, of which the Balmont set, Opus 6, are particularly grateful specimens.

(10)

Turning from the Petrograd School to that of the old capital, once associated with conservatism, we find a perfect galaxy of progressive young composers all distinguished, like their northern *confrères*, by an all-round culture, but devoting themselves rather more closely to the piano, an instrument whose literature has been greatly enriched by them.

Of these the *doyen*, so to speak, is Evgenie Gunst, who, as his name suggests, is of German extraction. He was born in Moscow in 1877, and studied Law at the University before embracing a musical career. His masters were Glière, Jilyaef and Goldenweiser. The fact that he has published a monograph on Skryabin might be accepted as a token of his discipleship, but in this respect his music is at present an even more convincing document. His compositions number two piano sonatas, deeply imbued with the Skryabinist spirit but lacking the master's constructive power, and he has recently turned his attention to Tagore, whose Sacrificial Song he has set. This work is said to reflect the influence of Wagner and Rimsky-Korsakof, which does not suggest the music one would expect as the complement of the Indian singer's poetry. One does not learn without some astonishment that the principal agent in the welfare of the Moscow Society for the propagation of Chamber-music has entered the dramatic region; but it would appear that the incidental music written by Gunst, for a work by Sologub, recently produced at the Kommissarjevsky Theatre, not only shows the composer in an entirely new light but suggests that this branch of the art is his true *métier*.

The brothers Krein, though both youngish men, have already earned something like a European reputation. Gregory, the elder (he was born in 1880), is the better equipped, having had a more liberal education. He first attended the Tiflis Music School, proceeding later to Moscow, where he studied the violin, taking the theoretical subjects with Glière. Subsequently he went to Leipsic, a most unsuitable school, one would say, for a progressive composer; but his choice of Reger as a teacher suggests a desire for a complete musicianship, and this Krein has certainly attained. Deriving much from Skryabin, his music contains a less spiritual and a more subjective emotionalism, which at times borders on sentimentality. His product is chiefly for piano, but the " vocalises," a form of Song without Words, in which Rakhmaninof has also experimented, have attracted a great deal of attention. A violin sonata, a recent effort, is spoken of as being his most powerful work and as affording abundant evidence that his creative individuality is now thoroughly established.

Alexander, born in 1883 at Nijni-Novgorod, also studied at the Moscow Conservatoire, the 'cello being his primary study. His early works for violin, piano and voice aroused great interest, and his approach to maturity was watched by the musical public with curiosity. The Balmont song, after Shelley, " I fear thy kisses, gentle maiden," composed in 1905, betrays a certain originality, and in its slender accompaniment there is no little warmth and poetic feeling ; but in the ensuing examples for piano there is an ever-increasing emotional power, and a harmonic richness that comes as much from the composer's own feeling as from any outside source. Quite lately he has come forward as a symphonic writer with a work of which the subject is Salomé. Its treatment is described as Oriental, but of a type distinct from the conventional Eastern idiom. From all accounts the music is of a provocative kind ; it has received a good deal of praise, but the critics are united in deprecating Krein's insufficient resource in orchestration, a study which the composer appears to have neglected. Among the many piano works are two series of Hebrew Sketches. There is a third brother, David, a distinguished violinist.

Skryabinist influence is again exhibited in the later examples, for piano, written by that composer's foremost literary champion, Leonid Sabaneyef, one of the first to expound the psychological content of *Prometheus*. Born at Moscow on September 19th, 1881, Sabaneyef was for some time a student at the University, but received nevertheless a thorough musical education from Zvieref, Shletser and Taneyef, all associated in one way or another with Skryabin. His compositions, which include a piano trio, Opus 4, and a violin sonata, Opus 12, are chiefly describable as miniatures, taking the forms of Prelude, Etude, Sketch and Impromptu. Of these the earlier specimens are somewhat wanting in individuality, especially in respect of harmony ; but the six Poems, Opus 11, are decidedly original. Their complexity does not repeat itself in the four Fragments, Opus 13, but its absence does not cause any diminution in the value of the latter series. The style is full of charm, the melodic figuration preserving a link with pianistic tradition which the harmonic material threatens.

Sabaneyef is a voluminous writer on musical æsthetics ; his articles are to be read in various journals.

The Younger Generation

With the art of the above-mentioned group, that of Nicholas Roslavets has little or nothing in common. Roslavets is a versatile composer and evidently a man of cultivated tastes and wide sympathies. At present, however, he appears to be wilfully singular and, whether intentionally or not, is exceedingly obscure and difficult. Originally a pupil of Abaza, at Kursk Music School, his music betrays an affinity with Schoenberg's, and will not, therefore, be expected to resemble the song of the nightingales with which that district is said to abound. It seems likely that he has been influenced a little by Rebikof, although he appears to possess a greater profundity than the latter. As to external symptoms it is worthy of mention that Roslavets affects coloured ink, a circumstance which will have some significance for students of latter-day tendencies ; more striking than this are the Cubist designs which adorn the covers of some of his pieces. Roslavets has a very marked and independent individuality, but lacks restraint.

One imagines him to be unable to curb the flow of a long-pent-up store of ideas, for there is a profuseness which, when added to the complexity of his writing, becomes positively forbidding. Among his youthful works are some settings of Verlaine's *Paysages Tristes*, which are of an accessible kind and less intricate than the songs to modern

Russian texts. There are some small compositions
for piano, and, besides a string quartet for the
conventional group, Roslavets has published a
Nocturne for an unusual combination consisting
of harp, oboe, two violas and 'cello, a work of which
the score is inviting. The piano and violin sonata
should also be mentioned, but the possibility of
extracting any value it may contain is remote,
since the fiddle part is quite unplayable. There is
no doubt that we shall hear more of Roslavets.

(12)

To Sabaneyef, whose literary gift is, as has been
said, considerable, fell the sad duty of chronicling
the death of a young musician whom he regarded
as " the talent of a century." His name has
already been mentioned in connection with one
of Medtner's last compositions, which is dedicated
to his memory. Alexis Vladimirovich Stanchinsky
was born in Vladimir in 1888, and was a pupil in
the Moscow Conservatoire. Sabaneyef's obituary
notice makes sad reading, recording as it does the
short life-story of an altogether abnormal being
whose last years were darkened by an affection of
the brain. His career had been watched by the
several eminent musicians whose attention had
been drawn to his wonderful gift, and the four
Sketches for piano, the only compositions published
prior to his death, had been recognized as the work

of a great genius. There have now been published in all eight sketches (Opus 1), but according to Sabaneyef there are two sonatas and a number of smaller works which may perhaps be issued. Informing these sketches is a simplicity and directness that recall Moussorgsky, but they are the work of one who speaks in a language whose vocabulary has accumulated a greater wealth and an increased subtlety. Stanchinsky died in September, 1914, and was interred in the cemetery at Novospasskoi, the birthplace of Glinka.

* * * *

A century has elapsed since the composer of *A Life for the Tsar* came into the world, appearing at a moment which preceded a new age in Russian national, social and musical life; Stanchinsky's death took place at a time at which the fate of his country was not easily to be divined, but which now seems to have been a preparation for an era of even greater portent. Even if it be granted that had this young artist survived, Russia might have been vouchsafed another mighty name with which to begin a new chapter in her musical history, the loss is far from being irreparable, for the musical prosperity of a nation is safest when in the hands of a community of gifted men, and, in its possession of numerous composers, each of whom is endowed with a considerable measure of genius, Russia has a good augury of future glories.

INDEX

Index

Index

Index

322

Index

323

Index

Index

325

Index

Index

Index

328

Index

329